Leading on the Edge of CHAOS

The 10 Critical Elements for Success in Volatile Times

EMMETT C. MURPHY
MARK A. MURPHY

Viva Books Private Limited
New Delhi • Mumbai • Chennai • Kolkata • Bangalore • Hyderabad

Original English language edition published by Learning Network Direct, Inc.

First Indian Edition 2003
Reprint 2007

VIVA BOOKS PRIVATE LIMITED

- 4737/23 Ansari Road, Daryaganj, New Delhi 110 002
  E-mail: vivadelhi@vivagroupindia.net, Tel. 42242200

- Plot No. 76, Service Industries, Shirvane, Sector 1, Nerul, Navi Mumbai 400 706
  E-mail: vivamumbai@vivagroupindia.net, Tel. 27721273, 27721274

- Jamals Fazal Chambers, 26 Greams Road, Chennai 600 006
  E-mail: vivachennai@vivagroupindia.net, Tel. 28290304, 28294241

- B-103, Jindal Towers, 21/1A/3 Darga Road, Kolkata 700 017
  E-mail: vivakolkata@vivagroupindia.net, Tel. 22836381, 22816713

- 7, Sovereign Park Apartments, 56-58, K. R. Road, Basavanagudi, Bangalore 560 004
  E-mail: vivabangalore@vivagroupindia.net, Tel. 26607409, 26607410

- 101-102 Mughal Marc Apartments, 3-4-637 to 641, Narayanguda, Hyderabad 500 029
  E-mail: vivahyderabad@vivagroupindia.net, Tel. 27564481, 27564482

Published by arrangement with

Learning Network Direct, Inc.
Subsidiary Rights Department
240 Frisch Court, Paramus
New Jersey 07652

ISBN 81-7649-367-8

Rs. 295.00

Published by Vinod Vasishtha for Viva Books Private Limited, 4737/23 Ansari Road New Delhi-110 002. Printed and bound at Raj Press, R-3, Inderpuri, New Delhi.

To

Carol and Andrea

CONTENTS

ACKNOWLEDGMENTS

This book is the result of a collaborative effort involving many people, including our clients, colleagues, and families.

First, we wish to express our appreciation to our clients. Their courage, intelligence, and commitment provided the solid research base of actual experience from which the content of this book emerged. Our work involves us with executives who are facing the real challenges of an increasingly volatile and chaotic economy. At a time when we search as a society for models of integrity and idealism in leadership, these men and women demonstrate the talent, resolve, and humility essential for success. Their encouragement and willingness to learn with us provided the key inspiration for the book.

Although there are too many to list everyone individually, the following people and companies deserve a very special thank-you: Larry Carter and Cisco; Howard Schultz and Starbucks; Meg Whitman and eBay; David Pottruck and Charles Schwab; David

Glass and Wal-Mart; Herb Kelleher and Southwest Airlines; Steve Ward and IBM; Robert J. Schuetz and William M. Mercer, Incorporated; Leonard Gray and Deloitte & Touche, LLP; Dale Morrison and Campbell's Soup Company; Robert Beyster, Ph.D. and Science Applications International Corporation; Koichi Nishimura and Solectron Corp.; Rita Garcia and Xerox; Elaine L'Esperance and M&T Bank; Jim Young and DuPont; Tom Silvestrini and Derrick Corporation; John Malone, Jim Pepicello, M.D., Don Inderlied, and the Hamot Health Foundation; and Leo Lopez and Critical Devices, Inc.

Second, we wish to acknowledge the support of our colleagues at the Murphy Leadership Institute, including our Washington, D.C. and Cambridge, Massachusetts research teams. The Washington team consisted of Michelle Thomas, Ph.D., Peter Kagan, Richard O'Toole, Ph.D., Janet Taille, and Jessica Zimmerman. The Cambridge team consisted of Melissa Calkins, Ph.D., David Cheng, and Kathleen Lattimore. In this context, we wish to express our appreciation for support and cooperation from the University of Rochester's William E. Simon Graduate School of Business Administration, the Massachusetts Institute of Technology's Sloan School of Management, and the American Management Association.

We would also like to express our special appreciation to two other colleagues and friends for their invaluable insights, Chris Pollack Ph.D. and Steven Wallace, Ph.D.

We are also indebted to Tom Power, Senior Editor at Prentice Hall, and his colleagues for their insight into the need for this book and their confidence in turning to us to write it. The whole process was guided by our friend and agent, Michael Snell, whose counsel is an ever-present source of support.

Most importantly we wish to thank our wives, Carol and Andrea, without whose support and love this book would not have been possible.

INTRODUCTION

"Long live technology"... "Technology is dead."

"Stocks surged upwards again today"...
"The Dow is down 400 points."

"The future looks bright"... "Hang on—it's gonna be a rough ride."

"September 11, 2001"...

Welcome to the new world economy of the twenty-first century. Do you have mental whiplash yet? If so, you should probably get used to it. Being a leader today is reminiscent of the polite Chinese curse: *May you live in interesting times*. You can definitely say it's interesting. And, you can also say it's volatile and chaotic.

In many ways, volatile and chaotic are together the perfect words to describe this new economy. Volatility describes the economy's rate of change: blindingly fast, with explosive upsurges and gut-wrenching downturns. Chaos describes the direction of the economy's changes: The familiar world we thought we knew has been replaced by a new order that we have yet to discern. The bottom line? We're not sure exactly where we're headed, but we're motoring back and forth between the various alternatives at speeds that would make a NASCAR driver sick.

Large, volatile swings define today's business environment: swings in fortune, in expectations for the future, in estimates of risk, in scientific and technological progress, in feelings of optimism, and in a post-September 11 world, our sense of security. One day, prospects for success fuel optimism and risk taking, and the next, world events or declining economic indicators induce heart-stopping fear. Uncertainty affects every industry—whether new economy start-ups, old economy titans, healthcare, banking, consumer cyclicals, energy, or utilities. No one has been spared. If anything, recent events have illuminated the web of interdependence that unites every sector of our economy, giving proof to the saying that "what happens anywhere matters everywhere."

Each new downturn takes the fortunes of companies and their leaders with it, while upswings leave many unprepared to ride them to the top. If the dot-com bust proved anything, it's that what goes up rapidly and unpredictably can come down the same way. To escape this fate, leaders must learn to stay ahead of the volatility curve and its inherent dangers. They must learn to manage rapid upturns as well as downturns. They must learn to anticipate and prepare for volatility, and discern patterns and order amidst the chaos.

Fortunately, there is a cohort of exceptional leaders who can teach us the strategies that ensure economic success, regardless of whether the economy is rocketing upwards, diving downwards, or fibrillating between the two.

In 1986, we began a research project to identify the characteristics of the world's most successful leaders. We called these leaders "benchmark leaders" and they established the criteria by which other leaders would be evaluated, and ultimately trained. The identification and study of more than 1,000 benchmark leaders, out of a field of 18,000 leaders, led to the publication of *Leadership IQ*. That project eventually grew into our current effort, and the Murphy Leadership Institute. In 2001, watching the economic turbulence and the uncertainty of world events, we revisited those benchmark leaders and identified a host of new ones, focusing especially on those who had achieved exceptional success in volatile times.

These high-performing leaders never forgot the reality of economic volatility—and they've never forgotten how to manage it. They understand that an economic uptick is not a cause for sloppy leadership. They also understand that a downturn is not a cause to abandon the quest for competitive success. They have learned how to succeed at "the edge of chaos," that zone of adaptivity and creative insight where complexity science tells us breakthrough achievement occurs. While their competitors wring their hands and flounder in the face of tumultuous change, these leaders have learned how to see the patterns in chaos and take charge. They've learned how to act boldly to safeguard their organizations and lead them to a brighter future.

We worked with these high-performing leaders to identify the ten greatest challenges of a volatile and chaotic economy. We listened to them, observed them, and analyzed our research data to see how they managed these challenges. Each chapter that follows focuses on one of the ten leadership best practices that emerged from this effort. To help you implement these proven strategies for success, each chapter provides concrete rules for action, illuminating case studies, and practical tools that you can begin using immediately to guide your organization through volatile times.

However, we want to pass along a caution that our benchmark leaders gave to us: implementing one or two of these strategies is no guarantee of success on all fronts. While the individual strategies provide proven solutions to specific challenges, their greatest value lies in the integrated protocol for leadership created by their fusion—a whole greater than the sum of its parts.

That protocol begins by understanding the need to *make haste slowly*. To survive in this volatile economy, leaders must move with greater speed and precision than ever before. This "need for speed," however, does not mean that leaders should act without first taking time to think. In fact, just the opposite is true. Leadership intelligence is more important than ever. If ever there was an economy that punishes sloppy thinking, this is it. Chapter

1 will help you turbocharge your thinking so you can move your organization quickly and in the right direction.

Second, partner with customers. Now, more than ever, customer satisfaction and retention are critical to success. But in times like these, many leaders become insular, ignoring customer partnerships to focus solely on internal operational challenges. As a result, they disconnect themselves from the best source of current revenue and future success. Chapter 2 will show you how to reconnect with customers to create a shared future that is more secure than either could have built alone.

Third, *build a culture of commitment.* The strength of an organization's culture is one of its most fundamental competitive advantages. Unfortunately, times of volatility will stress your culture to its limits. If you can build and preserve a culture of commitment, one where employees passionately pursue the organization's mission, you can come through volatile times not only intact, but better positioned for success. Chapter 3 shows you how to strengthen your culture by creating a shared sense of purpose and aligning rewards and incentives appropriately.

Fourth, *put the right person, in the right place, right now.* Exceptional leaders know they will have to assemble and align the right collection of talent to face the challenges that lie ahead. Therefore, they select, de-select, hire and fire to create a high-performing team with a wide range of talents. Chapter 4 will show you how to invest your human capital to maximize individual, team and organizational success.

Fifth, *maximize knowledge assets.* Managing knowledge assets is one of only three processes for which the now legendary Jack Welch took personal responsibility. Why? In a knowledge economy, an organization's ability to harness and maximize information plays the dominant role in creating competitive advantage. Chapter 5 will teach you how to identify, mobilize, and create knowledge assets so you can boost the value of your organization's intellectual capital.

Sixth, *cut costs, not value.* In a turbulent economic environment, any company can experience slowed revenue growth, lowered earnings, and overall weakened financial health. There's no shame in having to cut costs, but there is grave danger in doing it incorrectly. Organizations that "cut the muscle along with the fat" can cripple their ability to survive and compete. In Chapter 6, we present proven rules for cost management that will help you reduce expenses while protecting and enhancing the value of your business.

Seventh, *outposition your competitors*. In a rapidly changing business environment, competition intensifies for an often elusive and sometimes shrinking market. Success goes to those who can understand and develop sources of competitive advantage. Chapter 7 will help you uncover, build, and leverage your organization's unique competitive dimensions.

Eighth, follow a proven recipe for inspiration—*stir, don't shake*. Successful leaders understand that the stress of living in "interesting times" can cause an organizational panic attack that can stop progress in its tracks. Therefore, they reduce anxiety and inspire hope by stirring employees to higher levels of achievement, not shaking them with negativity and fear. Chapter 8 shares techniques that will help you manage stress without losing that "competitive edge."

Ninth, *cut through the noise*. Benchmark leaders understand that chaos and what physicists call "noise" rise in tandem with volatility, undermining a leader's ability to communicate. Without the ability to communicate effectively, a leader's other skills are worthless. If you can't communicate, you can't partner with customers, build a culture of commitment, or implement any of the other strategies for success. Chapter 9 provides you with a five-step protocol to get your message through the noise.

And tenth, *focus or fail*. To implement the key strategies and manage all the other challenges that can emerge in volatile times, leaders need a blueprint for action. Our study revealed that highly effective leaders follow a carefully structured process that focuses their energies while highlighting and prioritizing high-leverage opportunities for success. Chapter 10 shows you how to implement this process step by step so you can stay focused and on track.

In the Epilogue, entitled "When Bad Things Happen to Good Corporations," we address what happens when crisis hits. The ten critical elements explored in this book provide a process of stabilization that helps to both reduce the risks of volatility and the likelihood of crisis. But even for great leaders and their companies, crisis is sometimes inescapable. Benchmark leaders know that while the exact timing of a crisis event isn't known, we can estimate its probability and learn how to prepare to meet it. The Epilogue provides a process for understanding, planning for, and adapting to crisis, including the special threat of terrorism.

Overarching the whole book is an important theme: Volatility and chaos aren't by definition bad or good. They are just realities. Volatility and chaos are not necessarily synonyms for strife, hardship, or discontent. To the extent that they are for some, they are also synonyms for breakthroughs, discoveries, and optimism for others.

Times of volatility and chaos can bring about fundamental changes—for better and/or worse. The fact that we can't yet discern exactly what those changes will be doesn't spell disaster. It simply means that we have to alter our strategies to prepare for whatever the world may bring next. In this new world, leaders must anticipate, rush to think, reach out, build enduring bonds with customers and stakeholders, and get comfortable with leading at the edge of chaos.

Getting Started

Before you jump into the book, may we suggest that you *make haste slowly*. As with all our work at the Murphy Leadership Institute, we believe the best place to start is with a self-assessment. While you may wish to jump right into reading the chapters, we recommend you take a few minutes to complete the mini Volatility Leadership Assessment in the Appendix. It will help you understand how you and your organization compare with best practice leadership strategies, and where you might find it most useful to focus your initial efforts.

CHAPTER ONE

MAKE HASTE SLOWLY

On the edge of a new millennium, on the brink of a new stage of human development, we are racing blindly into the future. But where do we want to go?

—Alvin Toffler
Future Shock

Maurice Greene is the reigning world champion in the 100-meter race and the world record holder in both the 60-meter and the 100-meter. In the 2000 Millrose games, one of the most illustrious stops on the U.S. indoor track and field circuit, Greene surprised many observers by winning the significantly longer 400-meter race by .05 seconds. When asked how Greene managed to edge out his competitors, Coach John Smith replied, "He took his time."

Smith's point was that Greene ran a smarter race as well as a faster one. Smith explains, "The 400 sucks up everything you've got, so you have to be very careful about how you distribute your energy throughout the race. You need to structure the race, and you need a plan." Smith helped his runner win by analyzing the race and finding the best path to victory. He found that as runners reach the last 20 meters of a race, they face the limits of exhaustion and their bodies start to fail. Those athletes who run the first stages intelligently, however, can conserve their energy for the finish.

"Sprinters are most vulnerable in the middle of a race, because they want to punch that accelerator," says Smith. "But if you hit it too soon, you'll run out of gas. You've got to give [it] enough time to unfold, so that you'll be in the best position to apply great force. People think that all a sprinter needs to do is to run all out, but . . . I want my sprinters to do just the opposite. I want them to show how easy it is to run fast."

The parallels between racing and leadership are obvious. Succeeding in today's volatile and chaotic environment can suck up everything you've got unless you develop a strategy to outpace your competitors. Consider the challenge: Waves of technological innovation have intensified competition and redefined the speed of business and will continue to do so. It took Microsoft almost 14 years to exceed annual sales of $500 million, but it took Netscape only about three years to reach that goal. Between 1993 and 1998, Web commerce grew from next to nothing to a $22-billion business. The average lifecycle of a PC has gone from 19.7 months in 1989 to less than 6 months now. As our ability to create more, better, and faster increases with every passing year, business leaders will have to move with greater speed and precision than ever before.

We might be tempted to think that this "need for speed" spells an end to careful thought as a fundamental requirement of leadership. We might be tempted to think that in times of intense volatility, and even chaos, leaders shouldn't "think," they should just "do." We might be tempted by these thoughts, but we would be dead wrong. If ever there was an economy that punished mistakes and a lack of critical thinking, this is it. We have been on the front lines with leaders dealing with volatile times, and we're here to report that thinking clearly and acting quickly are more important than ever before. And that means that *leadership* is more important than ever before.

To win in today's economy, organizations need leaders who can help them run fast by showing them how to run *smart.* Through the rules that follow, the high-performing leaders in our study will show you how to speed up by taking time to think.

Rule 1: Resist the Lure of "Ready, Fire, Aim"

If you're reading this book, you already know that the clock is ticking; we don't need to beat the whole "new economy moving at Internet speed" thing to death. It's a given that product development cycles are shorter, competitive advantages emerge and disappear in the blink of an eye, and companies rise and fall with unprecedented speed. Like it or not, when the whole world speeds up, you have no choice but to kick into the next gear.

Unfortunately, many people think that speeding up means eliminating processes like "thinking" or "planning" or "aiming." In a recent interview, Herb Kelleher of Southwest Airlines, one of the great CEOs of our time, was quoted as saying, "The way you have to be in the airline business is ready, fire, aim, because if you take too much time aiming, you never get to fire."

Kelleher isn't alone in his sentiments. A recent search on Yahoo! for the phrase "ready, fire, aim" yielded over 3,000 responses (and narrowing the search criteria revealed that the majority were business-related). There are even several books available that reinforce the idea that "aiming" is a waste of time, and that survival in this newer, faster economy requires a steady diet of "fire, fire, fire."

Of course, the obvious counter to this argument is that many of these "fire, fire, fire" companies have only succeeded in shooting themselves in the foot. In its long run of profitable business, however, Southwest Airlines has not. Clearly, Herb Kelleher has found a way to fire at the right targets. What is his secret?

With all due respect to Mr. Kelleher, he *is* aiming—he's just aiming faster and better than most of his colleagues. Like Kelleher, most highly talented people cannot describe exactly how they work their artistry. Would Beethoven have been able to write *Symphonies for Dummies*, or would Einstein have penned, "The Theory of Relativity in 10 Easy Steps"? To understand geniuses at work, you have to analyze their performance—and that's exactly what we've done with our high-performing leadership group. To see how they aim, let's return to that interview with Herb Kelleher.

Rule 2: Aim at Multiple Targets—Now

In the same interview, Kelleher also said, "I'm prepared for all possible scenarios of what might happen. I usually come up with four or five different scenarios. I do this all the time. I do it in the shower. I do it when I'm out drinking. Right now I'm thinking through the scenarios of the possibility of United Airlines and American dividing US Airways. . . .You have to think that way all the time."

Does this sound like someone who doesn't aim? Or does it sound like someone who is constantly analyzing and planning—aiming at targets his competitors can't see, just waiting for the right moment to fire? A great leader like Kelleher demonstrates that leaders shouldn't wait until they have a problem to start aiming. Kelleher thinks ahead to the most likely scenarios, so when something happens, he's poised to take advantage of it.

Ron Dembo, CEO of Algorithmics, Inc., and a leading authority on the risks of modern business life, has also found success with this approach. A former Yale professor, he now creates risk-management software for banks, insurers, and other large corporations. Dembo describes his views on "aiming in advance": "When it comes to risk, the most common error that people make is to think about the future in terms of a single scenario. Why? Well, look at the newspapers; listen to the analysts. They're full of predictions: 'Interest rates will be lower.' 'Internet stocks will crash.' 'The Dow will go down.' These so-called experts have no idea what's going to happen. Never confuse a forecast with a scenario. . . ."

Algorithmics had one major client in the early days, a large commercial bank that provided 80 percent of its revenue. Because the bank had such a close relationship with the company, they helped fund and direct product development. One day, the bank decided to exert its influence and force Algorithmics to make major changes in its business model. Dembo says, "Its executives figured that because they represented 80 percent of our revenue, we would do as they asked. But because we had managed our risk, we didn't need them as badly as they thought we did. So we parted ways with them." Wisely, Dembo had forecasted this scenario, and had kept head count low enough to ensure survival in case of the client's defection. Today, Algorithmics is one of the world's largest risk-management software companies, and Dembo owes his success to always having a "Plan B."

As Henry David Thoreau once said, "In the long run, people hit only what they aim at." In a volatile and chaotic economy, nothing is certain; therefore, high-performing men and women must take aim at a variety of scenarios so they can quickly hit the ones that will bring success.

Rule 3: Pace Yourself

With the need to aim at multiple targets and react quickly, you might think you should be running constantly. But as track-and-field coach John Smith points out, no one can run flat-out all the time. In fact, to the uninitiated, sprinters appear to waste a lot of time. Their workouts focus on stretching and resting, interrupted by a few minutes of maximum exertion. Smith explains that world-class runners use their downtime to recover, so they can really perform during the seconds that matter.

So, too, do world-class leaders. Even in highly volatile times, there are moments of downtime. High-performing leaders seize these moments to catch their breath and take aim at the next set of opportunities. As the body goes into rest mode, the mind kicks into high gear, developing a strategy for winning the next race.

Helping companies take time to plan has been key to Jeff Levy's success. Levy is founder, president, and CEO of eHatchery, an incubator firm that helps technology companies get up to speed before the speed of the marketplace catches up to them. Using a structured process, Levy helps new companies work through the chaos of a company launch to take aim quickly and well. During the first month of its contract with eHatchery, start-ups must complete a survival checklist; they then act on those objectives, develop a marketing plan, develop an offering, test and refine it, and then obtain funding. As Levy explains, "It doesn't matter how fast you run if you're not heading toward the finish line. When you're working 24 hours a day, and ten people are doing 100 tasks in one room, it's easy to race pell-mell down a blind alley."

Rule 4: Find a Center That Can Hold

Who are we? Why are we here? What are our values? What is our purpose? These are weighty questions, often explored by philosophy majors in late-night dorm-room sessions. But if you think these questions are the sole domain of existentialist philosophers, think again. "Who are we and why are we here?" are essential questions for every organization, especially those facing turbulent times.

Several studies have found that companies that enjoy long-term success have a clear sense of their mission and core values; together, these things provide a guiding purpose for the organization. These high-performing organizations keep this purpose fixed, even in the midst of a whirlwind economy and fundamental market shifts. James C. Collins and Jerry I. Porras, authors of the book *Built to Last: Successful Habits of Visionary Companies*, noted that truly great companies understand the difference between what should never change and what should be open for change, between what is genuinely sacred and what is not. Their study found, and our studies confirm, that organizations that successfully manage change in the outside world develop an unchanging "center" that holds the company together when everything around it is flying apart. As Collins and Porras put it, "An effective purpose reflects people's idealistic motivations for doing the company's work. It doesn't just describe the organization's output or target customers; it captures the soul of the organization."

The "soul" of an organization isn't a new or radical concept. In 1960, in a speech to Hewlett-Packard employees, David Packard said, "I want to discuss why a company exists in the first place. In other words, why are we here? I think many assume, wrongly, that a company exists simply to make money. . . . You can look around and see people who are interested in money, but the underlying drive comes largely from a desire to do something else . . . . to do something which is of value."

Clearly, an organization cannot succeed in the long term if it does not contribute something of value to society. But what about the short term? How can purpose and values help you move quickly? Dawn Gould Lepore, Vice Chairperson and Chief Information Officer of Charles Schwab Corporation, puts it eloquently: "The velocity of change in today's economy requires a steady commitment to your fundamental values. If you don't have something that your employees can hold on to, everything is up for grabs and people lose their way. We constantly tell our employees, here's what's changing—and there's always something changing—and here's what isn't changing: who we are and what we stand for."

Finding a center that can hold helped VeriFone Inc. negotiate several major changes and emerge triumphant. The company, which developed the ubiquitous little gray boxes for processing credit card payments, rocketed from revenues of $31.2 million in 1986 to more than $600 million ten years later, trouncing all competitors along the way. What held the company together through rapid growth, intense competition, and an eventual merger? In a word, *values*. VeriFone doesn't have just a mission statement; they have a mission book that states the company's eight guiding values in seven different languages. As one manager said, "The backdrop of this culture is a sense of urgency, immediacy or 'we need it now.' Everything is a priority, by definition, but you need to prioritize, otherwise it becomes a panic. . . . We're making important decisions, and we have to look at them in context."

For successful organizations like VeriFone, the context for making fast and solid decisions is its living book of guiding values. In a volatile economy, high-performing leaders recommend that you take the time to develop your own "book of values" before you race to do anything else.

Case Studies: Bringing the Rules to Life

Throughout the book, we use storytelling to illustrate how companies have put the rules of our high-performing leaders into practice. In each chapter, we select two leaders and/or organizations that exemplify the rules, and then show how they dealt with volatility or some other business crisis. For this chapter, we have selected IBM, that, despite its size, knows how to run smart *and* fast. We have also selected Delphi, a manufacturer of catalytic converters, to show how even traditional "old economy" industries can reconfigure themselves to compete nimbly in a fast-moving world.

IBM: The Speed Team

In November of 1999, Steve Ward, Vice President of Business Transformation and CIO at IBM, decided that IBM needed to accelerate the way it did business to keep pace with the competition. The next morning, IBM's speed team was born. Ward called together 21 employees who had led innovative projects that were completed unusually quickly. Then he gave them a "simple" assignment: Get IBM's information technology (IT) team—more than 100,000 people worldwide—on the fast track to develop Web-based applications.

Karen Ughetta, team member and town hall meeting coordinator, says, "A lot of people hear that word [speed] and think that we want them to keep doing the same thing, only faster, harder, and for longer hours. But we're really about getting people to change the way they do things, about blowing up the process and discussing ways to avoid speed bumps."

Jane Harper, one of the team's co-leaders and Director of Internet Technology and Operations, explains IBM's strategy. "Every day, we do really good things in this company. We wanted to know why some projects happen more quickly than others. But then we wanted to look at those smaller projects and ask, 'What were the barriers to speed?' We started calling those barriers 'speed bumps.'"

After sharing their experiences and analyzing fast-moving, successful projects, the speed team uncovered six critical success factors for speed. The six attributes are strong leaders, team members who can work quickly and well, clear goals, effective communication, a process for carrying the team forward, and an accelerated agenda. Underlying all these attributes was one common idea: If you want to go faster, you need to respect time. High-performing (and fast) teams recognize that time is a resource, just like people, money, and materials. If you are serious about working quickly, then you need to measure time as much as you measure these other resources.

However, while measurement is important, overly rigorous measurement can be a major speed bump. "People complained about breaking down the 13-week projects into 13 phases and having to produce measurement reports at the end of each week," says Karen Ughetta. Team co-leader Ray Blair also cites the company's application development as one that ultimately slowed things down rather than sped things up. "One size does not fit all," he says. Rather than comply with the corporate bureaucracy, "speed demons," as IBM calls them, follow their mission by complying with the spirit of the law rather than its exact letter.

Based on its findings, the team recommended several quick-win strategies that made an immediate difference in the way IT staff work, as well as long-term initiatives that require changes in policies and procedures. Some of the quick wins included creating a speed rating in employee performance reviews and asking all leaders to articulate their time priorities. Long-term plans will address the working relationships between finance employees who fund projects and team leaders who run those projects. At IBM, the speed team has successfully shown everyone that time really *is* money.

In the fast-paced world of technology, leaders have a special responsibility not to use the "ready, fire, aim," school of leadership. Application development is so intense and expensive, with such far-ranging implications for users, that technical leaders must aim, and aim well. However, no other sector of the economy moves as fast, so leaders must also aim quickly. Like John Smith, IBM's speed team analyzed the factors necessary for success. They then infused the values of speed into the corporate culture, providing a center that could hold as a large organization underwent immense transformation and acceleration.

Delphi: Fast Converters

Today, Delphi Automotive Systems Corporation prides itself on unused office space—about 500,000 square feet of it. Back in 1997, Delphi used all of its 1,000,000 square feet of floor space to produce catalytic converters using an assembly line. However, its customers, the major automakers, began demanding customized converters. They also began to cut down on the number of suppliers, choosing vendors who could handle multiple tasks. These market forces demanded that Delphi reinvent itself—and quickly.

Today, the Oak Creek, Wisconsin plant has cut its need for floor space in half, eliminated 230 processes, and increased productivity by more than 25 percent. The key to Delphi's success was quickly transforming itself into a fast-paced, flexible production powerhouse.

Of course, the changes did not happen without some trauma, and they did not happen overnight. In fact, it took about six months for employees to buy into the need for change. However, in the automotive industry, which is heavily unionized, that process actually went quite fast. It helped that organized labor supported the transformation. Rick Warridge, a union representative, says, "We were quite arrogant. We used to own the market. But with competition, customers would be able to dictate what they paid for our product. Since many companies build catalytic converters now, the threat of a strike wasn't a reality. We either had to work together or bury our heads in the sand."

Working together, Delphi managers and employees moved from the standard assembly-line method of production to one based on "work cells." Recognizing that living objects provide the best model for speed, flexibility, and adaptation, plant leadership redesigned the manufacturing process to resemble a biological cell. Each cell requires between one and four workers to make a converter, and is supplied by a conveyor belt that brings supplies on a just-in-time basis. The conveyor belts, machine tools, and robotic components that are used to assemble converters are all built from modular components. Every piece of equipment can be broken down and reassembled on the fly in case surprise orders come in or a problem occurs. In the old system, people worked around the assembly line. Now the assembly line works around the people.

Because the new process is flexible and adaptable, the people who build the product can brainstorm ideas for improvement. Machine operators are no longer drones performing the same monotonous tasks all day long. Instead, they manage quality control, establish assembly speed, and suggest innovations that lower assembly times. As a result, automakers can place an order for customized converters on Monday, see it roll off the "assembly cell" a few days later, and receive it by the end of the week.

At Delphi, the only thing that's now inflexible and frozen is an old assembly line that workers have had "bronzed" to remind them of how far they've come from their formerly slow ways of thinking and working.

Many "old economy" businesses that traditionally "hit what they aimed for" have had difficulty adapting to the new speed of business. In recent years, many tech companies have sped into the future, only to reap the harvest of having fired before they aimed. Delphi was able to integrate "fast" and "smart" aiming by pacing themselves and using employee involvement as the center of their transformation. By involving key stakeholders in the change effort, Delphi built the momentum at the start of the race that would carry them through to the finish. Had they "jumped the gun" and attempted to make the changes without the support of their workers, they might never have reached the finish line at all.

Practical Strategies For Making Haste Slowly

Case studies and stories can be inspiring and entertaining. Sometimes, however, it's hard to decipher how you can apply their lessons to your particular situation—not the most helpful tactic in rapidly changing times. Therefore, in each chapter we draw out some practical strategies that every leader can use immediately to emulate the success of the leaders in our study. Here are the strategies that will help you run smarter and faster:

- **Watch the clock.** The ultimate competitor in any race is the clock. All companies, like all runners, race against time. If you accept time as the ultimate standard of winning or losing, then you need to hold yourself accountable to that standard. This means including time as a resource and performance metric in your evaluations, hiring, and project management, just as IBM did.
- **Watch your competitors.** The obvious competitors in a race are the other runners. Without competition, it's a parade, not a race. To succeed at that race, you need to keep an eye on your competitors at all times, analyze what works and what doesn't for them, and find a way to set your performance apart.
- **Watch yourself.** Ultimately, you compete against yourself in every race. Success boils down to how well you can manage

your physical stamina, your mental toughness, and your "zone of performance." John Smith says that you can tell when someone has run a blazingly fast race: The person is smiling and claims it was easy. High-performing leaders are tough and competitive, but they never forget that the race is about setting challenges, finding the reserves within yourself, being true to your purpose, and crossing the finish line smiling.

A Parting Message: Rush to Think

We conclude each chapter with one clear, compelling thought that encapsulates the practices of the leaders in our study. If you can't remember all the rules, or you forget the stories, our parting message will help you come away from the book with a summary strategy for managing volatile times.

For this chapter, our parting message is that successful leaders *rush to think* before they rush to act. They carefully size up the competition, take aim at a variety of targets, consider possible scenarios, and create a plan for getting from start to finish. As they make haste slowly, they consider all the components of the organization that must be mobilized for success: customers, knowledge assets, operating costs, organizational culture, and communication, among others. We urge you to "rush to think" about these issues as well in the chapters that follow.

Ready, set, go!

CHAPTER TWO

PARTNER WITH CUSTOMERS

Giving people a little more than they expect
is a good way to get back more than you'd expect.

—Robert Half

At the Storage Decisions 2001 conference, a gathering of executives from the data-storage industry, Joe Tucci, the CEO of EMC—the world leader in data storage—asked for a show of hands of how many people thought EMC's salespeople were too arrogant. Of the 400 attendees, around 150 raised their hands.

This wasn't anything new to Tucci. When he took over as CEO in January 2001, it was amidst an economic slowdown, slowing revenue growth, increased competition from groups like IBM and Hitachi Data Systems, and increasing complaints about EMC's our-way-or-the-highway attitude. In years past, EMC's storage systems were so far ahead of the competition that if customers were put-off by the attitude, there wasn't much they could do. In fact, it was this technological dominance, and the ensuing business success, that gave rise to the attitude. But now, with competitors' products every bit as good as EMC's, the attitude had to go. At the conference, Tucci said, "If there's anything I disdain, it's arrogance. Clearly we have to address that." And address it he has. EMC has greatly reduced the number of clients that sales reps service, so that each rep spends considerably more time listening to, and understanding the needs of, customers. Quotas have also been reduced to further reinforce the message and ensure proper alignment of the organization's people architecture. There have also been several terminations, particularly among the most arrogant salespeople. Tucci summed up these moves simply: "You've got to weed out the rotten ones."

While it's still too early to pronounce the ultimate success or failure of Tucci's efforts, customers thus far seem to have noticed a change. One customer who asked not to be named noted, "Rather than telling me what I will take, my rep now works with me to figure out what I need. He sees me as a partner and not a target. Rather than telling me what they will and won't do, he says 'Push us to our limits. Tell us what you need and we'll move mountains to make it happen.' Regardless of why they got their wake-up call, I do think they got it."

In turbulent times, no force is more grounding and stabilizing than a partnership with customers. The customer is the foundation of the organization's success. In a pluralistic, open-market economy, the customers are the principal source of power, voters who "vote" with their wallets and feet. Creating a partnership with customers helps organizations maintain the focus they need to make good decisions and harness the power and commitment they need to weather volatile times.

However, it's important to remember that "turbulent" doesn't just mean "bad" times. When the times are good, it can easily be forgotten that customers hold the key to your success. Too many companies with technically-superior products or protected markets get carried away with those advantages during boom times by dictating to, rather than partnering with, customers—and, as evidenced by EMC, that strategy only works for so long.

Models of Customer Partnership

What exactly does partnering with customers mean? Individual leaders have very different definitions of this concept. To demonstrate this point, we turned 53 CEOs into test subjects. During a recent "Leading a Turnaround" program at our corporate retreat center at Seabrook Island in South Carolina, we replicated an experiment from the *Leadership IQ* research project, asking the CEOs in attendance to draw how they saw themselves in relation to their customers and their organizations. The responses ranged from stick figures to complex engineering-style blueprints, but three major models emerged:

- **The egoist.** Egoists viewed all of their relationships as one-way information transfers. When egoists had something to communicate, they expected that everyone around them would listen and agree. Even with customers, this type of leader dictated the who, what, when, where, and how of their products and services. As was evidenced in the beginning of this chapter, EMC was a classic example of this model.

- **The bureaucrat.** Bureaucrats saw themselves and their employees as hierarchical and insulated from their customers. They focused almost exclusively completely on internal structures and relationships, to the point of not even including customers in the picture. Too often, the bigger an organization gets, the more susceptible they are to this model. That's one reason why so many government agencies fit in here.

The Egoist

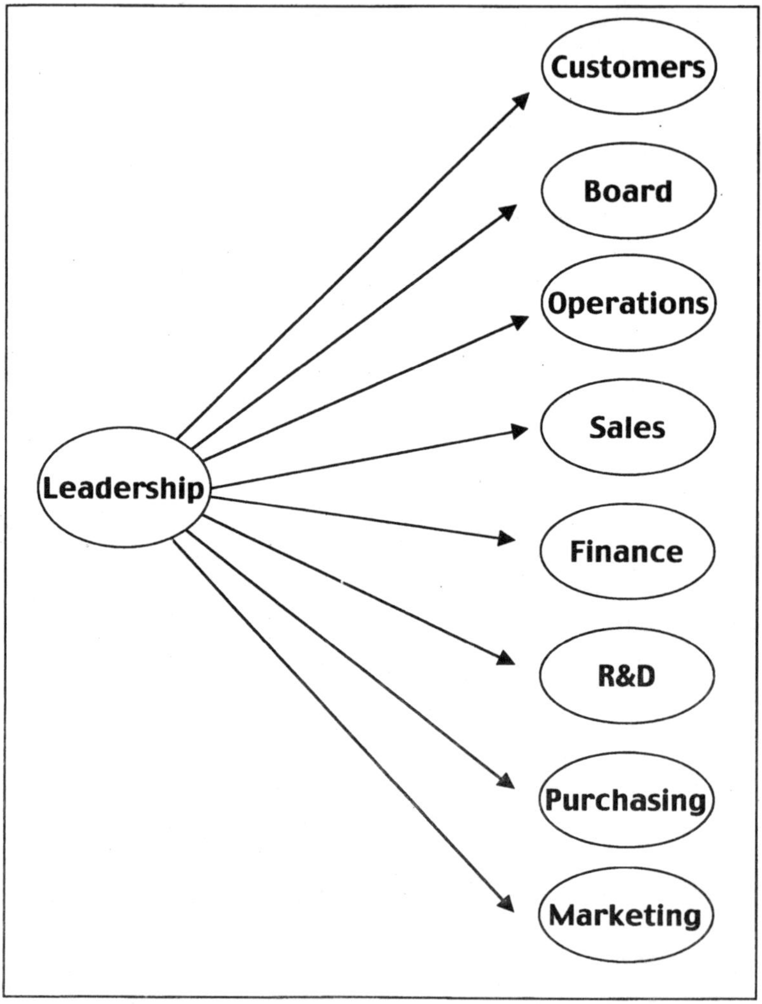

- **The Customer-as-Partner (CAP) model.** The last group of leaders viewed themselves as engaging in a two-way dialogue with the customer. In focus-group discussions, they verbalized a strong sense of responsibility for beginning and maintaining that dialogue. Many of these CEOs drew themselves as moving outside of the organization to bring the customer into a partnership with the organization—not just senior leadership, but with every person and department. CAP leaders believed

The Bureaucrat

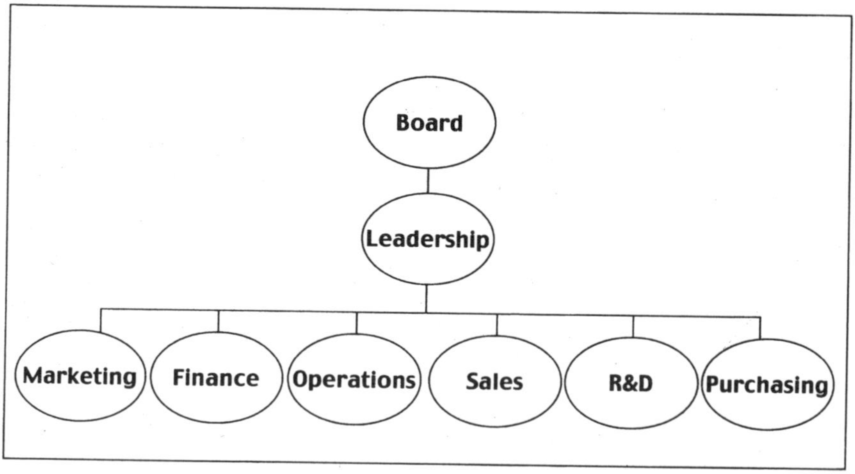

The Customer-as-Partner Model

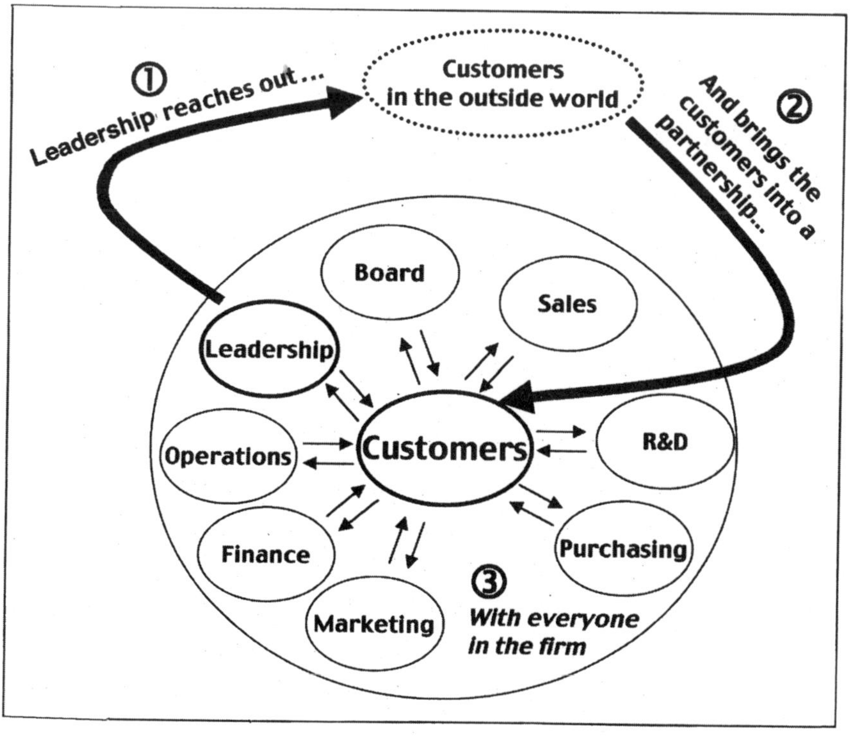

that the customer influences every single area in the organization, and therefore every department must partner with customers.

The CEOs at this conference were about equally divided between those who were new to turnaround situations and those who had had previous experience. While all of the participating CEOs were committed to doing "whatever was necessary" to effect a turnaround, some had an innate advantage. Fully two-thirds of the experienced turnaround specialists viewed themselves as CAP leaders. The numbers were reversed in the other group, with less than one-third seeing themselves as CAP leaders. Interestingly, these numbers closely parallel what we found in the Leadership IQ study: successful leaders adopt a view of the world that is closer to the Customer-as-Partner model than to any of the others. As we followed the success of leaders in turnaround situations, those who were committed to the CAP model produced 3 times the profitability during the twelve months following the conference as the others.

How Does the CAP Model Drive Success?

Our exercise at the retreat, and the research that followed, reconfirmed our conclusions from the original *Leadership IQ* research. While we had always known that the Customer-as-Partner model distinguishes highly effective leaders from their colleagues, we now had a better idea of how that model drives success in volatile times.

The CAP model recognizes the dynamic relationship between organizations and their customers (unlike the other models, which show either a static or unidirectional view of the world). Highly effective leaders realize that organizations and their customers depend on each other for their mutual success, especially in a volatile economy. Customer partnership is more than "putting customers first" or finding mutually satisfactory solutions to shared problems. It requires not only a dedication to excellence in every sale or service encounter, but also a commitment to forging long-term relationships that create synergies of knowledge, security, and adaptability for both parties. *Customer partnership is a shared journey to create a future for both parties that is better than either could have developed alone.*

Partnering with customers strengthens the bonds of customer loyalty that organizations need to survive and prosper in turbulent times. Consider the following statistics:

- Acquiring new customers can cost five times more than satisfying and retaining current customers.
- The average company loses 10 percent of its customers each year.
- A 5-percent reduction in customer defection rate can increase profits by 25–85 percent, depending on the industry.
- The customer profitability rate tends to increase over the life of a retained customer.

The message is clear: Customer retention and satisfaction drive profits. It's a basic notion, but one that bears repeating, especially in volatile times. When resources are scarce, leaders tend to look inside their organizations for solutions like cost cutting and productivity improvement. While these activities are important, it is equally important to look outside the organization for solutions that only customers can provide. Understanding customer needs helps leaders define new market opportunities, and drive innovation and revenue growth in every aspect of the organization. It also helps them meet current market challenges and anticipate future market shifts. In a rapidly changing world, customer partnerships count more than ever before. The following rules demonstrate how to create them.

Rule 1: Make Partnership Everybody's Job

One of the key points of the Customer-as-Partner model is that the customer influences every aspect of the business. Of course, everyone knows that customers drive sales, revenue growth, and mar-

CAP Operational Checklist

R&D:

- Do staff regularly, proactively, and directly involve customers in the R&D process to ensure they are meeting their needs?
- Do R&D staff seek out feedback from other departments (e.g., Marketing and Sales) during the product development cycle?

Sales:

- Do sales staff actively feed information to other departments (e.g., Marketing, Operations, etc.) regarding changing customer needs?
- Do salespeople share information about customers among the team, or are they territorial?

Marketing:

- Do marketing staff continually identify new areas of buyer need?
- Do they constantly suggest new offerings for new or existing customer segments?

Purchasing:

- Do purchasing staff make their purchasing decisions based upon customers' needs rather than their own (e.g., not compromising quality for price)?

Finance:

- Do finance staff respond quickly to customer needs?
- Do they use billing and collection strategies that build customer relationships instead of straining them?
- Do they understand the profitability of various customers and customer groups?

Operations:

- Do operations staff continually strive to improve the quality/speed/cost of the product or service?
- Do they understand how the end-user utilizes their product or service?

ket share. However, it is not so obvious that customers should drive R&D, purchasing choices, manufacturing decisions, and even accounting and finance. Ultimately, an organization exists to serve its customers, and that recognition should permeate every process, department, and job role. For that reason, partnering with customers cannot be left to isolated departments like marketing or customer service. Everyone in the organization, from front-line employees to the Board Chairperson, must find ways to connect with customers.

While it may not be feasible, particularly in a larger organization, for every single employee to speak directly with customers, there is no reason why everyone can't see the results of customer satisfaction surveys, market research, e-mail inquiries, complaint letters, etc. This information can help individual employees perform better in their own roles and make greater contributions to cross-functional customer partnership teams.

The checklist below will help you determine the extent to which customer partnerships exist throughout your organization. Ask yourself to what extent employees in each area involve the customer in key decisions and processes.

Any question that receives a negative answer is an opportunity to bring that particular department or division into closer partnership with customers.

Rule 2: Partner with Potential Customers

When we talk about partnering with customers, we often overlook the "dark matter" in the customer universe—potential customers—existing in large numbers, typically unseen, yet wielding an enormous power. These are the people who are not currently using your products or services; people who think they have no use for the services in your industry or who consciously choose another company's product or service over yours.

Partnering with potential customers is an activity that shouldn't be postponed until the economy heads south. In good times, it's too easy to adopt the attitude that "all the people who *really* know what's happening are using our product/service, so if you don't like us, it's your problem, not ours." Yahoo! offers a wonderful example of this phenomenon. As the Internet boom kicked into high gear in 1998 and 1999, Yahoo! was besieged by companies begging to advertise on its site. With this success came an attitude of entitlement and conceit. Yahoo! was a "new economy" company, on the "cutting edge," and the old rules didn't apply to them.

Thomas Evans, the CEO of GeoCities, a company acquired by Yahoo! in 1999, warned his Yahoo! counterparts, "Ad sales are cyclical. . . . People hate you. You're arrogant and condescending. When there's a downturn in the market, they'll cut you first." These warnings were quickly rebuffed by Yahoo! President Jeffery Mallet, who allegedly said, "You don't get it. You're old media." In early March 2001, when Yahoo! warned it was going to severely miss first-quarter earnings and revenue projections, blame was placed squarely on the weakness of advertising sales, and CEO Tim Koogle and Anil Singh, chief sales and marketing officer, quickly announced their resignations.

High-performing leaders recognize that potential customers represent a tremendous opportunity. After all, there are two main ways to grow revenue: Either increase your share of current customers' wallets (See Rule #4) or increase your share of the overall market. If you want to pursue the latter strategy, you need to understand why potential customers aren't buying your products or services.

Uncovering this information can take a variety of forms, from market research surveys to focus groups to special incentive offers (e.g., free trials, gift certificates, etc.) to thorough postmortems on lost sales. For example, while advising a large advertising agency that was losing a significant number of bid competitions, we discovered that very few of the partners were doing postmortems on the lost sales. Instead, they assumed they knew why they were losing. Yet, when they acted on those assumptions and did things differently, nothing changed.

When this firm called us in, the first thing we did was to conduct a thorough postmortem on a recent lost bid. Several of the partners were surprised to learn that most of the people to whom they had submitted their bids were more than willing to share why they chose another firm. Very simple questions like "Would you mind sharing what particular factors drove your choice of ABC?" and "For future reference, would offering XYZ have made a significant impact on your decision-making process?" generated a wealth of information. The postmortem told us what was driving the recent losses, and four more postmortems confirmed the news. Based on our analysis, the firm immediately changed the way it communicated its new consulting strategy and won its next bid. Through the basic act of analyzing lost sales leads, this advertising agency gained the knowledge it needed to convert potential customers into actual ones.

Rule 3: Partner with Lost Customers

In times of volatility, lost customers may be the most important group of all. Losing customers can be very dangerous, with every lost customer creating a domino effect until there is a mass exodus from your company. Unfortunately, customer retention is especially difficult today, as our digital culture has taught consumers that they can switch loyalty with the click of a mouse. Customers bring that expectation to every sales encounter, whether your organization is a technology pioneer or a corner grocer.

To head off a potential customer stampede, leaders must find innovative ways to partner with lost customers. Not all of those customers will return, but the lessons learned in the process can prevent future losses. Most important, preventing the loss of even one customer can help break the negative cycle of customer defection, where the bad experience of one customer contaminates the loyalty of the rest.

As with potential customers, leaders can partner with lost customers in a variety of ways. The most important rule to remember is: Never let disenchanted customers walk away without the equivalent of an "exit interview." In fact, when important customers walk, it is not out of the question for senior leaders to meet with them directly. The key is to avoid defensiveness or bullying the customers back into the fold. Rather, empathize with their decision and find out why they're leaving. Ironically, showing this level of concern and understanding—without trying to recoup lost business—may actually win back some of your lost customers. Often, these lost customers are actually seeking a deeper partnership with you and threaten to walk away as a "test" of your commitment.

For example, when Vic Babel of Babel Paints was looking for space for a new design center, he offered the building owners an ultimatum: Kick out two tenants so I can take over their space, or I won't sign the deal. When the owners readily agreed, Babel got up and left the negotiation table. As Babel explained, "They'll do the same to me for the highest bidder." Babel tested the owners' commitment to other customers as a gauge of how they would treat him, and found that the customer partnership he needed was lacking. Imagine the synergies the building owners could have created if they had worked with Babel and the other tenants to create a long-term mutually beneficial relationship for everyone involved.

Rule 4: Increase Wallet Share

Building partnerships with customers can reveal new opportunities to grow revenues and enhance customer service. Known as "increasing wallet share," this strategy means discovering untapped needs that open up exciting market opportunities. Especially in a turbulent economy, where the costs of acquiring new customers can be more than five times higher than generating more revenue from current customers, increasing your share of your current customers' wallets can reap huge benefits.

Increasing wallet share often requires offering new or augmented products or services, but the payoffs can be significant. Consider Callaway Golf, maker of the famous Big Bertha golf clubs (of which, in the interest of full disclosure, we must say that one of the authors is a devotee). Through customer partnerships, Callaway Golf realized that their customers often pondered which golf balls to use with their new Callaway clubs. Seeing an opportunity to expand their product offerings, and thus their revenue, Callaway designed a series of golf balls. On the five major professional tours combined worldwide, the Callaway Golf ball became the number-two brand of golf ball in just one year, with more than 150 professionals putting the ball into play in 2000. In addition to seeing a new market opportunity, Callaway realized that they weren't fully maximizing the value of one of their biggest assets—their brand name. While being careful not to stray too far from their core mission, and thus diluting their brand name, they saw an opportunity to use an existing asset to generate additional revenue (and profit). Especially in a volatile economy, squeezing every drop of potential return from the assets you already own is critical.

When Nike partnered with their running customers, they realized that not only did runners need running shoes and apparel, but they also needed heart monitors, MP3 players, and sports watches. Nike developed these offerings and their equipment business now boasts sales in excess of $400 million. GE's Power Systems and IBM partnered with customers and greatly increased their wallet share with a wide range of consulting and maintenance services. As long as the products and services are consistent with the organization's mission, increasing wallet share can be a great way to harness the power of customer partnerships.

Even nonprofit organizations can increase wallet share. In healthcare, for example, labor and delivery is typically a relatively low-margin area of hospital operations. Many hospitals have even had to close L&D units to focus their attentions on more cost-effective services. However, innovative organizations maintain the delivery of obstetrical care by increasing revenues through the sale of "premium" services to those who can afford them, including high-end baby photography, mother's helpers services, and deluxe accommodations and in-room catering.

Rule 5: Let Go of "Poor Fit" Customers

Paradoxically, during times of economic uncertainty, the smartest approach to profitability may be to let some customers go. Normally, customer defection should raise alarms, but there is one group of customers whose defection shouldn't concern you—the unprofitable customer. These customers demand so many resources from your organization that they actually end up costing you money. Unprofitable customers may represent only a small portion of your business, but they tend to drain a large share of attention and resources from more profitable business lines. In times of high volatility, "firing" unprofitable customers can be a great cost-savings device that helps strengthen partnerships with profitable customers. (Of course, we recognize that some industries, like healthcare, can't easily turn away non-paying customers.)

Another paradoxically successful strategy is to turn down potential business. Some customers may look profitable in the short term, but will become unprofitable in the long term because they are a poor match with your organization's mission. In seeking sales, leaders sometimes forget that it is just as important for customers to be a "good fit" with the organization as it is for employees. As tempting as it may be in a volatile economy, selling products or services that are inconsistent with your capabilities is a bad move. If you manage not to lose money throwing more and more resources at the customer's unreasonable demands, you will lose future sales when the customer leaves, dissatisfied, and begins to bad-mouth the organization.

Unfortunately, no formula can determine which potential customers will become unprofitable. Making that call requires a "gut check" against your mission. The big tip-off: You find yourself treating your customers, your principles, or your employees with less integrity than they deserve. Case in point: A small municipality hired a struggling architectural consulting firm to help with a federally funded construction project. The president of the firm agreed to take on the customer without disclosing that they had never worked on such a large and complex project before. He then assigned one of the most talented, but least seasoned, associate to manage the project. In short order, the municipality lost the federal funds and thus the chance to complete the project. Then the firm found itself facing a malpractice lawsuit for the full amount of the lost multimillion-dollar federal contract. Although the municipality eventually dropped the suit, several key associates resigned and the firm took a major hit to its credibility in the marketplace.

Even—and perhaps especially—in a volatile business environment, you should ask this question: Does this customer need services that we can or should offer in the spirit of our mission and values? If not, it may be better to let that customer go elsewhere. Then when that customer needs your services, or knows someone else who does, you will benefit from the competitive advantage of integrity.

Case Studies: Bringing the Rules to Life

To dramatize the rules of customer partnership, we've selected two different case studies. The first comes from the volatile and financially challenging world of healthcare, where the quality of customer partnerships can determine the survival of both organizations and their customers. Because we are still actively involved in an engagement with this client, we present their case study under a fictitious name.

The second case study shows how even an organization with a "captive audience" customer base can find new ways to partner with customers for enhanced growth. Our spotlight organization, the U.S. Mint, manufactures the coins that everyone in America touches. Despite a lack of obvious rivals in its "market," the Mint found ways to compete against its own past performance and, in so doing, reinvigorated its reputation and profitability. Together, these organizations illustrate the formidable power of customer partnerships.

University Medical Center: A Stitch in Time

Several months ago, we met with 200 clinical managers from one of the country's most prestigious teaching hospitals, which we'll call University Medical Center. Like many healthcare organizations, this hospital was facing declining revenues, market share, and patient satisfaction. We began the meeting by asking managers this question:

"If you can only pick one, do you think patients at this hospital would rather receive . . .

1. Care that is delivered in a timely fashion?
2. Care that is the most technologically and medically advanced?
3. Care that is delivered with a great deal of personal sensitivity?"

Intriguingly, a show of hands revealed a major lack of consensus. Approximately 40 percent of managers believed their patients primarily sought technologically advanced care—not surprising given the organization's mission. The remaining managers were about evenly divided between sensitivity and timeliness. This exercise told us two things: (1) These managers had no shared understanding of their patients' needs; and (2), clearly, nobody was asking the patients what they wanted.

In this case, management confusion about priorities translated into operational complexity and lack of focus. For example, those managers who believed that patients wanted technologically-advanced care pursued that goal single-mindedly. They purchased the most up-to-date equipment, integrated the latest research into daily treatment regimens, and freed up employees' time to read the appropriate journals, etc. By contrast, managers who believed that customers wanted highly sensitive care invested in staff training programs dealing with this issue. Those managers who believed in the marketing power of efficiency focused on trying to shave off minutes from key processes. As a business, healthcare is complex enough. This organization did not need three distinct groups of managers scattering the energy of the organization in different directions.

Our previous customer research, which in healthcare alone exceeds one million subjects, had revealed that expertise, sensitivity, and timeliness are all key indicators of satisfaction. However, some of these indicators hold more weight than others in particular settings. Shortly after this meeting, we conducted a customer assessment to find out exactly what this group of patients cared about. We found out that the patients at this hospital valued two aspects of care more than others: the timeliness with which the care was delivered (e.g., no more two-hour waits for blood work); and sensitivity, believing that employees cared about them as human beings, not just customers who needed things "done to" them. In other words, 50 percent of the managers were wrong.

These findings explained why an increasing number of patients had been patronizing several smaller competitor hospitals. While these smaller competitors were less high-tech, they were more high-touch and efficient.

Armed with an understanding of their customers' needs, hospital leadership developed a plan for meeting them. The hospital streamlined several processes, particularly those processes focused on patient treatment and hand-offs, including admissions, testing, and procedure scheduling. These activities, coupled with training programs that reminded staff about the importance of sensitivity, helped University Medical Center to recapture its lost customers and increase its market share.

Hospitals often exemplify an unfortunate legacy of many public service organizations and other companies—airlines, utilities, and even some high-tech firms, among others—that believe customers "need" their services. These organizations tend to become somewhat self-righteous and overconfident about their relationships with customers, because they see an unending demand for their services and view their customers as passive recipients rather than active partners. Unfortunately, any organization can fall prey to this complacency. Whatever their industry, high-performing leaders remember the basic fact that customers always have choices.

When University Medical Center recognized this lesson, they made partnership the job of everyone in the organization. They partnered with their current customers, realizing that this approach is often the best way to also influence potential customers and lost customers. Nothing reaches these two groups like positive word-of-mouth referrals from existing satisfied customers. When leaders recognize that customers partner with each other, fulfilling any one of the five rules makes it that much easier to follow the other four.

Philip Diehl and the US Mint: Making Change

Government agencies usually aren't recognized for their innovation—that is, until Philip Diehl became director of the U.S. Mint. When Diehl started at the Mint in 1994, the agency looked like a holdover from the Industrial Revolution, and a poorly managed one at that. In addition to making 20 billion coins per year, one of the critical functions of the Mint is to monitor the number of those coins in circulation—yet the Mint had no automated tracking system. Trying to match production to demand was a haphazard process at best.

Even more antiquated was the customer service center that took mail orders for collectibles and commemoratives. Employees crowded together in cramped rooms in a converted warehouse with a defective heating and cooling system. The mail order shop shared space with the U.S. Postal Service, which called a bomb threat and evacuated the building every time they encountered a suspicious package—up to several times a day. This Dickensian environment produced terrible customer service, with the average order taking more than eight weeks to fulfill. Employees were either warming up, cooling down, or waiting for a bomb threat to pass—no one had time to answer the phone or process orders. Even worse, "there was no sense of urgency about the problem, or even that there was a problem," recalls Diehl, who has since left the Mint with the change in presidential administrations.

Of course, it was no accident that the Mint was so disconnected from its customers. In fact, it was forbidden to communicate with them. Prior to 1992, the Office of Budget and Management (OBM) discouraged agencies from spending money on some of the more common customer service tools available to businesses—market research, focus groups, and customer satisfaction surveys. If you were able to push through the red tape and insist on using a customer survey, it first needed to pass a six-month OBM approval process. Frustrated, Diehl decided to contact his customers personally.

Diehl "went undercover" as a coin collector at coin conventions around the country and chatted with fellow collectors about their needs. Through his personal focus-group research, Diehl discovered the cause of the Mint's declining revenues and prestige. The "eight-week to infinity" delivery process for coin orders, coupled with the Mint's strict prepayment policy, meant that customers had to send their money into limbo waiting for a product that might never come. Naturally, most customers were reluctant to do so. Explains Diehl, "Most people at the Mint, and especially the people in customer service, believed that their job was to protect the assets of the U.S. government. . . . Before we send you your coins, we're going to make sure that your check clears. . . . We really believed that customers were trying to defraud the government. Today, we have gone to the other extreme—the customer is king."

With a new vision in place, Diehl convened a task force that established performance goals more suited to private industry than a government agency. Although modest at first, these initiatives touched off a wave of improvements at the Mint, including a migration to the Web for order processing. After implementing its customer service goals, the Mint gained permission to participate in the American Customer Satisfaction Index and found itself ranked second in the U.S., just after Mercedes-Benz North America.

However, Diehl was not satisfied with merely improving efficiency. Diehl and his team began to rethink not only how they did business, but also the nature of the agency itself. They concluded that the Mint was not just in the money business, but in the education and relationship business. Coin collecting, after all, is more than a hobby; it is a way for generations of families and friends to forge stronger relationships while learning about history. Diehl explains, "Coin collectors have always known that coins have two functions in society. Primarily, coins facilitate commerce. But also important, coinage has always been used to tell the story of our nation to its own people." Marketing Director David Pickens, reflecting on the stodgy nature of the federal agency, adds, "We had forgotten the magic in our product."

To recapture the magic, the Mint launched its most successful initiative to date—the 50 State quarters program, which like most changes at the Mint, was suggested directly by customers. The results have been phenomenal. Diehl explains: "How many companies have introduced a product that will sell more than 4 billion units in its first year and be touched by every person in the country?"

Philip Diehl clearly demonstrates the importance of making partnership everyone's job. As a civil servant nearing retirement, he could have let the Mint cruise along with the status quo. Instead, he personally chose to circumvent the barriers to customer partnership and build relationships with his customers. Like the leaders at University Medical Center, he was able to leverage a renewed relationship with current customers to recapture lost customers and gain new ones.

Practical Strategies for Customer Partnership

Both University Medical Center and the U.S. Mint faced potentially disastrous customer migration. To turn the situation around, they followed the five key rules using similar core strategies for customer partnership. You can use these strategies to build and strengthen your customer relationships, regardless of your industry:

- **Honor those who serve.** Both organizations were only able to partner with customers after they improved employees' working environment or integrated customer partnership into their culture. In doing so, they demonstrated a central truth: Partnerships with customers are only as strong as partnerships with front-line employees. Organizations that tell customer service people to treat customers as partners—but don't role model that behavior with their staff—exhibit the most dangerous form of organizational schizophrenia.
- **Harness the power of perception.** As these case studies demonstrate, perceptions of customer needs drive management decisions. Poor managers may simply ignore what customers need. Mediocre managers will attempt to serve customers based on assumptions. Only high-performing managers will take the initiative to discover what customers want and then provide it. But perhaps more important, they share those needs throughout the organization. This data provides everyone in the organization with a clear set of guiding principles that will help them stay focused in the midst of volatility and chaos.
- **Institute small changes for huge outcomes.** When leaders build partnerships with customers, every little action can create a significant outcome. As our spotlight organizations demonstrate, small beginnings and "quick wins" can create a snowball effect in an organization. Once employees begin to understand the value of customer partnership, they begin to seek out more opportunities to do so.
- **Find the "magic" in your products.** Magic is the ineffable quality that all customers want but few receive. In fact, it's become fashionable lately to talk about providing "customer delight." However, most organizations find that "magic" and "customer delight" are still beyond their capabilities. The reason: They attempt to identify basic levels of customer need, but they never develop the partnerships that uncover

customers' higher-level needs for meaningful interactions. Only high-performing organizations go beyond "useful" to "meaningful." For University Medical Center, meaningful service meant sensitivity and timeliness. For the U.S. Mint, it was recognizing the soft side of hard currency.

A Parting Message: Seek the Next Level of Service

As we revisit the messages of this chapter, one theme becomes clear: While the Customer-as-Partner model drives organizational success, it is more than a picture on a piece of paper. It is also more than a CRM system, customer relations training, or other form of customer "program." Benchmark leaders recognize that customer partnership is an ongoing relationship to seek the next level of service—new customers, new knowledge, new markets, and new products.

To illustrate this point, let us turn to one last exemplary leader. Bruce Antonelli is truly a leader with "heart." He's the Chairman and CEO of Necco, Inc., the company that specializes in the candy message hearts that everyone seems to give or receive on Valentine's Day. Despite widespread consolidation in the candy industry, through good times and bad, Necco has been successful for nearly 100 years. Necco's secret: customized production and packaging for any customer who requests it. Their competitors almost universally refuse to partner with retailers to reach specialized consumer markets, evidencing the take-it-or-leave-it attitude previously adopted by EMC and Yahoo! But Necco never walks away from a special request. As Antonelli says simply, "Hey, I'll talk to anybody. That's what keeps us growing." And in a volatile and chaotic economy, that's what it's all about.

CHAPTER THREE

BUILD A CULTURE OF COMMITMENT

A purpose is the eternal condition of success.

— Theodore T. Munger

"Has Enron become a risky place to work? For those of us who didn't get rich over the last few years, can we afford to stay?" When Sherron Watkins, Enron's Vice President of Corporate Development, wrote these words in a memo to former Chairman Kenneth Lay, she couldn't have known the historic role her words would play. What she did know, was that Enron had lost its way.

In fact, Enron had lost its very soul—its fundamental purpose and reason for being. It's tough to know what, exactly, caused this. It may have been the off-balance sheet financing, the Byzantine web of derivative financing, the complicity of their auditors in the implementation of dubious financial strategies, a recruiting strategy that relentlessly pursued arrogant and one-dimensional financial whizzes, or a morally suspect executive suite. But whatever the cause, we do know that at some point Enron became culturally hollow.

Enron, driven by its senior leaders, became a company without a cultural, moral, or emotional center. Words like commitment, customers, purpose, and values had no place in the corporate lexicon, much less in corporate actions. Executives exhibited utter disregard for employees and stakeholders. There was no corporate "superego" that put real checks and balances on Enron's executives. Self-serving greed was rampant. There was no sense of purpose or of working toward something bigger than an individual's needs. Executives' interests were clearly not tied to the best interests of the organization as a whole. In short, there wasn't commitment.

Leaders who have actually survived and thrived amidst real turmoil know that without a cultural center, without commitment, there is no way to succeed. Whether the challenge is preventing an Enron-like collapse, or recovering from one, successful leaders use commitment as a beacon for attracting, retaining, calming and focusing their people. One such leader, a CEO who recently led her company out of serious financial trouble, told us "A committed culture is the most important thing in a company. If we had constructed a culture based solely on stock price or on prestige, there wouldn't be a reason to be here now. At the end of the day, the thing that drives people through pain and turmoil is the belief that the world is a better place because of what they do."

Generating commitment isn't just for critically-ill organizations. Even if your organization has nothing in common with the Enrons of the world, your culture's levels of commitment can still be seriously tested by times of volatility. One economic downturn can be frightening and depressing, but an economy that swings from good to bad to worse and back again will push your people to their emotional limits. When those limits are pushed, even top employees evidence increased turnover and decreased productivity. These emotional swings can also make it more difficult to attract new talent into the organization. And in a volatile economy, the last thing a company can afford is for their best people to leave and be unable to attract new ones. Like the old submarine test in which a sub is put into deep water to test the integrity of its seals and gaskets, immersion in a turbulent economy will test whether your organization will hold together or implode under the pressure.

High-performing leaders understand that the "seals and gaskets" that hold an organization together is *commitment.* Commitment is one's dedication to others in the pursuit of values and beliefs. As St. James said, "Faith, if it has no works, is dead." Readers may be familiar with the more modern adaptation of this insight: "You can talk the talk, but can you walk the talk?" In other words, organizations can talk all they want about mission and values, but if they don't back that talk up with action, those values never come alive.

Perhaps nowhere else in organizational life do we see a greater gap between faith and works, or talk and walk, than in corporate culture. Nowhere else do leaders pay more idle lip service, and nowhere is lip service more transparent, and ultimately harmful. In fact, hypocrisy is sometimes worse than not having values in the first place—even heartless SOBs can get points for authenticity. Because a culture that lacks commitment also lacks the ability to bring its values to life, it will suffer from all that follows—frustrated employees, poor performance, absence of new talent, and dissatisfied customers.

In a Committed Culture, however, employees are devoted to fulfilling the organization's mission while working towards achieving its vision. A Committed Culture is one that, especially in turbulent times, aligns the individual interests of employees with those of the organization and its customers. Because a Committed Culture helps employees find a sense of meaning in their work, they are loyal, hard working, fulfilled, efficient, and passionate. Not surprisingly, Committed Cultures have lower undesired turnover, fewer labor problems, lower labor costs, greater numbers of satisfied customers, and a greater ability to manage change. And for all of these reasons, Committed Cultures are also magnets for attracting the best and brightest talent. The rules that follow will show you how to harness the competitive advantage of a Committed Culture in your organization.

Rule 1: Assess Your Current Culture

The first step to building a Committed Culture is to assess your organization's status and then identify ways to move towards commitment. We have found that high-performing leaders measure two broad dimensions of culture: purpose and people architecture.

Measuring Purpose

Purpose is the sum and integration of mission, vision, values, and passion. It is the extent to which employees understand and share the organization's vision, and the passion they feel about their contribution to the vision.

To measure an organization's purpose, leaders must ask two questions. First, what percentage of employees truly understand the mission and values of the organization? Second, what percentage of employees agree that they are worthwhile? When these two percentages are not high and/or relatively equal, an organization's purpose is unclear and confused.

For example, an organization may have employees who understand what the organization stands for, but feel those values are not consistent with their own. This type of organization suffers from a lack of purpose because its employees' hearts are elsewhere. Conversely, an organization may have employees who don't understand the organization's values and mission, but if they did would find themselves in agreement. That's a Committed Culture waiting to happen. However, it needs to be nurtured with better communication, involvement, and attention.

Measuring People Architecture

People architecture is the alignment between the organization's purpose and its reward and evaluation systems. To measure your organization's people architecture, first take an inventory of the reward and evaluation system used to motivate employees. Then consider the extent to which these systems support your mission, vision, and values. If these two issues are not aligned—i.e., if the incentive system contradicts the organization's purpose—then the culture will not hold together. When an organization encourges actions that are inconsistent with its mission, it becomes like a car with both the brake and the gas pedals depressed at the same time. At best, the car goes nowhere. At worst, serious damage occurs.

The Commitment Grid

The different combinations of purpose and people architecture create four different types of cultures. The commitment grid provides a way of thinking about these types and diagnosing where your organization falls.

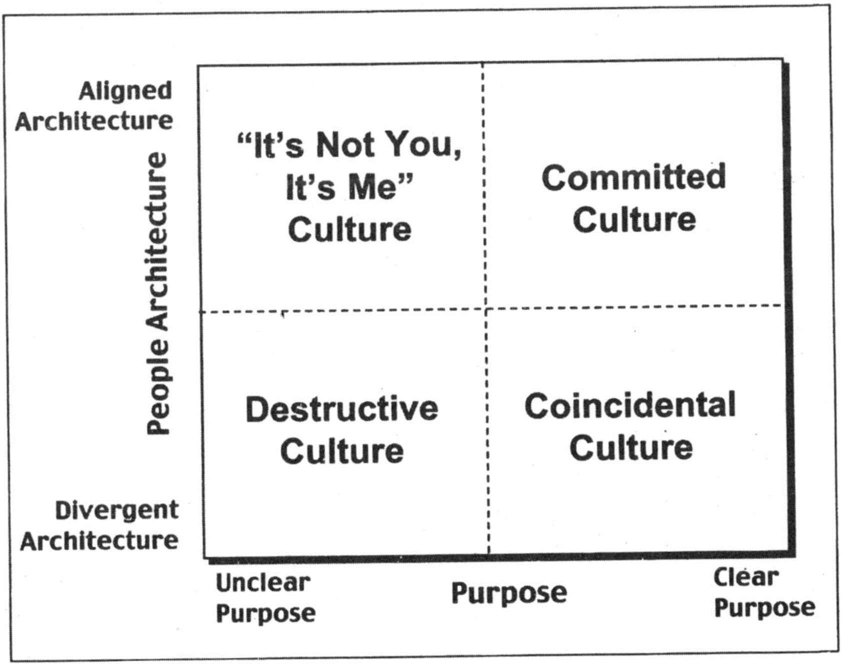

When most employees do not share a sense of purpose, and the organization's people architecture does not elicit the appropriate behavior, a *Destructive Culture* emerges. A Destructive Culture is usually marked by high staff turnover (particularly top talent), difficulty in attracting new talent, high labor costs, and low staff satisfaction and morale. While an organization might be able to limp along with this culture for very brief periods during calm times, there is just no way to survive with it in volatile times.

The *Coincidental Culture* is one with a high sense of shared purpose, but with an inadequate or contradictory people architecture. We call this culture type Coincidental because employees remain at the organization through no intentional effort on the part of leadership.

Many hospitals exhibit a Coincidental Culture. For as long as hospitals have existed, only a select few have had evaluation and reward systems that motivate staff to hit performance targets, whether patient satisfaction, clinical outcomes, or profits. Instead, hospitals tend to rely on the intrinsic values and passion of their dedicated staff to deliver high quality.

This type of culture can work well when employees don't have anywhere else to go. In the past, for example, if you offered most healthcare professionals the choice between working at an organization that reflected their values, or going somewhere that doesn't reflect them but offered them moderately more money, most would have opted to stay. But, as the healthcare industry has grown and evolved, these healthcare professionals no longer face an either/or choice between purpose and rewards. Instead, they are able to find jobs where they share a sense of purpose, and incentives reward them for living that purpose. This is one reason why hospitals face so many staffing shortages in key roles like nursing. Nurses can live out their purpose in a variety of settings, including settings far away from traditional hospitals, and receive greater reward.

A Coincidental Culture spells real trouble in turbulent times. Because it has little, if anything, holding it together, it can fall apart at the first little bump—and whether that bump is an upsurge or a downturn doesn't really matter. As long as the organization is no longer coincidentally heading in the same direction as the staff, the two will part ways and the organization is history.

The *"It's Not You, It's Me" Culture* was so named after the famous dating breakup line. It means that "you haven't done anything wrong, but we just don't fit well together." This culture occurs when employees understand the mission of the organization and are encouraged to achieve, but their personal values and beliefs do not mesh with their job requirements. It would be unusual to find this problem on a widespread basis throughout an organization; for this reason, "It's Not You, It's Me" is usually found in small pockets. However, when these pockets multiply, or wield significant power (like the executive team), they can destabilize the entire organization.

For example, this type of culture often arises when new leaders try to create a new purpose that runs counter to the existing one, or when hiring systems fail to select people with the right values. Al "Chainsaw" Dunlap, former CEO of Sunbeam, is a classic example of the "It's Not You, It's Me" problem, a new leader who cast aside the values and vision that had driven the organization and its employees for many years—with disastrous consequences. By ignoring the values of Sunbeam and conducting an unbridled downsizing, he disenfranchised an entire workforce.

In contrast to all of the other culture types, the *Committed Culture* merges both purpose and people architecture to create a culture where people understand and believe in the vision of the organization, and are encouraged and rewarded for making it happen. Examples of this culture are GE in the era of Welch and Wal-Mart in the era of Walton and Glass, as well as the case studies that follow later in this chapter.

Where does your organization fall on the Commitment Grid? Depending on its current placement, you may need to work on purpose, people architecture, or both. In this section, we'll talk about some of the drivers of purpose and people architecture, and how to align them.

Rule 2: Create a Shared Purpose

Several factors go into creating a shared purpose, including employees' understanding of the organization's values and vision, agreement with and passion for those values and vision. The following steps show how high-performing leaders incorporate these factors into their cultures.

Define Values

The first of these issues—ensuring understanding—requires an organization to have clearly defined values. Many organizations find themselves rudderless when it comes to their sense of who they are and what they stand for (above and beyond creating shareholder wealth). Without this, organizations can get themselves into real trouble. First, most employees, especially the really talented ones, need to know who you are and what you're about. Given how many hours they spend at work, and the important role it plays in their lives, talented people are looking for a "values fit" with their employers. Without it, they won't work for you. They'll leave. Second, values define what is and isn't acceptable—they become the organization's code of behavior. And making decisions without a code of behavior, particularly the kinds of decisions that are often required in volatile times, can be much more difficult and even dangerous.

Therefore, the first exercise is for leadership to engage employees in creating a list of the values that define what the organization stands for. Not only does this fulfill the needs outlined above, but it can be a powerful bonding exercise for leaders and staff. In turbulent times, creating a bond that could help retain your best people might mean the difference between success and Chapter 11. For example, MindSpring, the Internet Service Provider that merged with EarthLink, created a set of 200 "value" words that described its commitment to customers, shareholders, and all employees. These values were so powerful, and provided such a strong bond linking every person in the organization, that EarthLink adopted them after the merger rather than imposing its own.

Defining values is more than putting words on paper, however. Most organizations have mission statements or values statements; yet many do not follow them. Other organizations, like Nike, create successful cultures through visual representations of their values: competitiveness, inclusiveness, and action. While you may never hear Nike's mission statement when you buy a pair of sneakers, you know what Nike is all about.

Admittedly, nonverbal communication of your mission is tricky to carry off. Therefore, most organizations define and reinforce their mission through some type of document or other formal language. Here are some additional techniques that high-performing organizations use to create a shared purpose:

- orientation and training programs that emphasize corporate values
- both structured and unstructured opportunities to socialize with colleagues and supervisors
- "storytelling" events and corporate histories that dramatize guiding values
- a unique, shared corporate language that reflects values (a common example is calling employees "associates")

Test the Values Statement

Once leadership creates a draft of the organization's values, it's a good idea to test them with employees. This not only prevents the "It's Not You, It's Me" Culture, but also provides a gauge of leadership connection to the front lines. Dieter Zesch, head of Chrysler, has received surprisingly warm praise from the UAW and other Chrysler employees. This reception is particularly remarkable given that his job is to turn around the floundering automaker, and that includes getting costs under control. One of the major drivers of his success to date has been his connection with the front lines. He communicates his understanding of the values that sustained Chrysler for many years, as well as his commitment to maintain and protect those values. Among the values he aims to protect and reenergize is Chrysler's design prowess. Ironically, this core value and distinctive advantage was abandoned as Chrysler's financial situation worsened. By reenergizing that key value, Zesch is re-mobilizing a collective sense of commitment.

Select People to the Values

The next major step in creating a shared purpose is to use corporate values and vision to select the right people. If employees don't feel their personal values and beliefs coincide with the organization's, the result will be an unhappy worker and an unproductive organization. Too many organizations incur the tangible and intangible costs of "poor fit" employees, simply because they weren't upfront or clear about the organization's mission and values. Other organizations are up-front about these issues, but don't focus enough attention on ensuring that prospective employees are a good fit.

To help ensure a good fit, high-performing leaders use techniques such as stringent screening programs for all applicants and "promoting from within" strategies that develop and tap the talents of those who already understand the organization's values. For example, "fun" is a core value at Southwest Airlines and a vital part of its screening process. Retired CEO Herb Kelleher says, "We hire for attitude and teach skills if we have to. The interviewing process may seem rather idiosyncratic to you, but there is a system to it. Here's an example. We had a group of pilot applicants, and we told them that we don't interview people in suits. They had to wear Southwest Airline shorts instead. And so there they were, they had their suit jackets and ties on, and Southwest Airlines shorts. Well, the people who were happy to do that we hired, and the people who weren't, we didn't."

Unlike Southwest, your hiring process may not require employees to take off their pants. Nevertheless, it should reflect the purpose that drives your organization.

Of course, goodness of fit isn't just an objective in hiring new employees, but an ongoing challenge with current employees, whether they just started or have been with the company for 30 years. Sometimes, this challenge requires leaders to recognize a bad fit and then move on.

Consider Paul O'Neill at Alcoa, who, before becoming Secretary of the Treasury, used safety as the driving performance measure in his business. Alcoa's accident record is about one-twentieth of that of its competitors, leading to fewer lost workdays and greater profitability than any other aluminum manufacturer. O'Neill tells the story of what happens to employees when they don't uphold the internal priority of safety:

> "An order of sisters in Texas sent me some correspondence, indicating they believed we had had an incident in one of our Mexican plants where people had been overcome by fumes, and had to be hospitalized. While no one was hurt, they said it was a serious situation and they said they didn't think I knew about it. I simply didn't believe it. But it turned out they were right, and it also turned out that the division president responsible for this business knew about it and had an outside report done, by an independent environmental consultant, God bless him. The report indicated that it was probably a temperature inversion, combined with carbon monoxide from forklifts inside the plant, that had, in fact, overcome people. The business unit president didn't share the report with company headquarters environmental and safety people, as he was required to do by policy. This is a guy who'd been with the company 28 years, who had grown businesses from $100 million to $1.5 billion, but when it was clear he had not shared what had happened, he was fired. . . . A company must live by its values."

Rule 3: Align the People Architecture

Creating a shared purpose is only half of building a Committed Culture. The other half is the alignment of the people architecture, including reward systems and evaluation systems. If purpose represents the "faith" or "talk," then people architecture represents the "works" or "walk." People architecture helps to drive specific actions, align self-interest with organizational interest, and attract, retain, and select talented employees. The following are some of the more common ways high-performing leaders align their corporate people architecture with their purpose.

Reward Systems

High-performing leaders often say that the only way employees will fulfill the dream is to share in the dream. Reward systems are the mechanisms that make this happen. However, reward systems are much more than just bonus plans and stock options. While they often include both of these incentives, they can also include awards and other recognition, promotions, reassignment, non-monetary bonuses (e.g., vacations), or a simple thank-you.

The first rule of designing an effective reward system is to *carefully align it with the values, mission, and vision of the organization.* Systems that reward behavior unrelated to the mission can play havoc with an organization. The problem is not that the organization's people architecture doesn't drive people's actions; rather, it drives them too well. To paraphrase an old adage, be careful what you encourage—you just might get it.

Take the case of a computer company that decided to reward its clerical staff for their typing speed, rather than the quality of their work. After the company installed software to track each person's total number of keystrokes per day, the secretaries began leaving books and other objects on their keyboard during lunches and breaks to boost their "productivity." Of course, they also began to type faster without regard for spelling errors. After a few months of typo-filled documents going out the door, the company sheepishly abandoned that reward program.

The second rule of thumb for an effective reward system is to *reward behavior that is under employees' control.* Tying incentives to uncontrollable events, rather than manageable behavior, only leaves employees frustrated. For example, in 1990, Dupont's Fibers division initiated a reward system based on incentive pay that was called "one of the most ambitious incentive pay programs in America." The plan required the division's 20,000 employees to put as much as 6 percent of their compensation into an at-risk pool. If the division hit certain profit goals, the employees would receive a multiple of those monies; otherwise, they would lose the money. Although there was every reason to believe the division would hit its targets, an unexpected economic downturn and rising oil prices (a key raw material) decreased expected profits by 26 percent. As it became clear that the division would not hit its targets and employees would lose their at-risk monies, employee unrest became so high that DuPont canceled the new reward system.

Not every organization and employee group is equally motivated by money. Nor are profits always the driving force in an organization. The key is to identify your organization's driving force and key values, and then find metrics to measure performance on those issues.

Evaluation Systems

Evaluation systems are closely tied to reward systems and, in fact, drive the type, level, and distribution of rewards. The key questions leaders must ask in designing evaluation systems are: Who do we want to evaluate (e.g., individuals vs. teams), and on what competencies and criteria do we want to evaluate? Do we want to evaluate employees on their ability to satisfy customers, to learn new skills, to generate profits, or something entirely different? Choosing evaluative criteria is very much an exercise in alignment. A committed culture cannot be created when employees are told the organization values one set of behaviors but measures another. In leadership, what and how you measure becomes a de facto statement of what you value and stand for. Especially in times of volatility, employees must know that you are willing to "put your money (and other recognition) where your commitment is."

At GE, for example, evaluation systems are geared to categorize four types of employees by their values and results. The first, and most desirable, group lives GE's values and gets good results. The second type lives GE's values and doesn't get good results. These folks are encouraged and given a second chance. The third and fourth types do not live GE's values. Regardless of whether or not they get good results, these last two groups will be asked to leave.

At Cisco, customer service is one of the company's driving values and thus a large part of their reward system. They survey their customers several times a year in order to quantify customer service performance and tie the results of the surveys directly to managers' compensation. If scores go up, so does compensation, and if scores go down, compensation does, too.

Similarly, at St. Francis Hospital, where sensitivity to patient needs is one of their driving values, they use patient satisfaction surveys to quantify their level of sensitivity. While these results are tied to managers' compensation, much like Cisco's managers, they also have a reward program in which patients can nominate particularly sensitive and caring front-line employees. Once a month at a hospital-wide staff lunch, nominated employees are honored in front of their peers with a plaque and a named donation to a charity of their choice. It's not personal monetary compensation, but at St. Francis it doesn't need to be. One recent winner described it as the most meaningful recognition he had ever received.

At the heart of all commitment-driven evaluation systems is assessment of service in support of the customer. This means both the external customer—those who buy goods and services from the organization—and the internal customer—the employees who provide service to each other. A dangerous problem emerges when either one or the other type of customer is left out of the evaluation process. This problem can occur when salespeople or executives are evaluated on their effectiveness with clients while ignoring coordination with internal staff who make such service possible. Or, it can happen when the external customer is excluded from a so-called 360-degree evaluation where linkage to the customer—and the issues of service and profitability that follow—are ignored in lieu of team dynamics.

Case Studies: Bringing the Rules to Life

The high-performing leaders in the two case studies we selected for this chapter are experts in creating a shared purpose and aligning their people architecture to that purpose. Although their individual strategies may differ, bothz organizations clearly defined their core values, attracted and retained the right people, and motivated those people to live out their values through properly-structured incentive programs. Here are their stories.

Koichi Nishimura and Solectron: A Rapid-Response Culture

Solectron Corp. is the world's largest and fastest-growing contract manufacturer, and one that delivers exceedingly high quality, having won two Malcolm Baldrige Quality Awards in the 1990s. Its chairman is Koichi Nishimura, who joined Solectron in 1988, just as business observers were heralding the end of American superiority in manufacturing. Instead, Solectron has grown to $6 billion in annual sales in outsource manufacturing, providing cost-effective and speedy production of laptop motherboards, cash registers, cell phones, and other computer products for such original-equipment manufacturers as IBM and NCR. Solectron's success strategy is to shorten the supply chain, enabling it to produce goods faster than overseas manufacturers.

Nishimura runs the company with two guiding values: "superior customer service" and "respect for individual workers." Solectron jointly carries out both values through a rapid feedback system that gives workers the information they need to exercise their own judgment in meeting customer needs. Solectron surveys customer satisfaction not yearly, not quarterly, but weekly. Managers post updated survey results each week at the front of every production line. The other part of the feedback system is a profit-and-loss statement for each production line, which managers also receive weekly. Armed with this data, each plant is authorized to implement its own production schedule with only one guideline: "You can't lose money." In letting plant managers run their plants as if they were their own business, Solectron keeps bureaucracy to a minimum. Both managers and line employees receive quarterly variable pay tied to plant performance. Solectron also provides employees with a stock-purchase option that has enabled employees, even part-time workers, to purchase more than a billion dollars' worth of its stock.

Solectron faced the challenge of integrating another organization into its culture when it purchased NCR's retail-systems factory in Georgia. After charting employee sick days, NCR's leaders realized that their unlimited sick-pay policies had inadvertently provided long-term paid vacations for a few employees who knew how to milk the system. The newly acquired subsidiary decided to make a change in the spirit of Solectron's "do whatever you want; just don't lose money" credo. Under the new plan, employees accrue a certain number of sick days per year. Now, however, they are allowed to claim sick days before or after a holiday, which was forbidden before.

Not everyone was happy with the new standard, however. About 4 percent of employees quit as a result of the merger and related changes, and another 2 percent were discharged for failing to meet the new standards. Nevertheless, the new policies boosted morale by weeding out those who did not share the organization's mission. The remaining employees knew exactly where they stood vis-à-vis the organization's values and literally had the motivation in front of their faces to do something about it.

As a manufacturing company that requires rapid turnaround and low costs to be profitable, Solectron has to balance the standardization of processes that drive efficiency with the employee autonomy that enables creative solutions to customer needs. Rather than complicate this situation with convoluted rules and formulas, Solectron sets minimum design standards for its employees: Serve customers, respect each other, and do whatever you want to fulfill those rules without jeopardizing our shared future. These simple guidelines make it easy for Solectron to maintain a culture of commitment even as it continues to grow and acquire other organizations with dissimilar cultures.

Dr. Robert Beyster and Science Applications International Corporation

Dr. Robert Beyster founded SAIC in 1969 by mortgaging his house and setting up shop next to a ballet studio in La Jolla, California. Beyster had been employed at a large defense contractor, but had become frustrated with its bureaucracy and its deference to the demands of outside investors. Other entrepreneurial scientists quickly joined Beyster, and soon the company was thriving on an influx of federal contracts in the field of nuclear power. Today, the company specializes in research and development, system integration, and software development not only for the government, but also for business clients around the world. SAIC employs more than 41,000 employees, mostly scientists and engineers.

Founder Robert Beyster now owns only slightly more than 1 percent of the company's shares; the rest are owned by employees, making SAIC the nation's largest employee-owned information technology company. SAIC is also one of the few employee-owned companies with liquid stock. In 1973, Beyster set up a wholly owned subsidiary to provide a market for buying and selling company stock. Over the past five years, the stock has averaged annual returns of over 30 percent.

One of the keys to the success of SAIC's employee-ownership strategy is its corporate philosophy: "Those who contribute to the company should own it, and that ownership should be proportional to that contribution and performance as much as possible." The other key to SAIC's success is that it makes its employees owners in ways other than the financial. In addition to its stock-based reward systems, the company has a participative culture that encourages employee involvement in decision-making and a horizontal management structure that distributes control to the lowest levels of the organization. For example, each of its more than 600 divisions manages its own marketing and profit margins with minimal guidance from corporate offices. This people architecture enables SAIC to respond rapidly to market changes. However, the right to carry out senior leadership activities brings with it senior leadership-level responsibility. If a line of business dries up, that division must make a rapid course correction, transfer to another division, or conduct its own downsizing.

Given this diversified and autonomous corporate structure, centralizing communication can be a challenge. Therefore, SAIC uses more than 20 different organization-wide committees to address issues of importance to employees, including healthcare benefits and cost-reduction initiatives. Committee representatives attend meetings of the Board of Directors and report back to employees at all levels and divisions.

Dr. Beyster credits SAIC's philosophy of total employee ownership with its competitive position in the marketplace. "Most of the competitors we've had in the last 30 years have disappeared. They've been absorbed and then the companies that absorbed them have been reabsorbed by someone else. So employees who stayed with those original companies have had three or four different sets of management, all with different objectives. And typically caring less and less about what the people in the original company were doing." Continuity of leadership and values have, instead, created a culture at SAIC that is committed to continued growth and success.

Clearly, not every business founder is prepared to relinquish his or her ownership of the company the way Beyster did. However, every leader should realize that—despite one's best (or worst) efforts—employees own the quality, efficiency, and effectiveness of their work. In very tangible ways, therefore, they own the responsibility for the company's future. Recognizing that fact, high-performing leaders like Beyster help employees wield their power wisely by aligning their best interests with those of the organization.

Practical Strategies For Building Committed Cultures

Both Solectron and SAIC express the importance of employee ownership as one of their guiding values, although they do so in different ways and to varying degrees. In addition to this similarity in values, they share several practical strategies for building committed cultures. You may wish to consider these strategies as you strengthen your organization's purpose and people architecture to weather volatile times.

- **Let form follow function.** The two companies in these case studies, as well as the numerous examples we've quoted throughout the chapter, use many different approaches for motivating employees, ranging from public "thank-you's" to financial incentives. Each successful strategy is an outgrowth of that particular organization's unique values, vision, and mission. Therefore, what works for one organization may not work for another, even in the same industry. In culture building, imitation and benchmarking are only the starting point, not the destination.
- **"Sell, don't tell."** Walter Shipley, Chairman of Chase Manhattan, attributes this saying to Ben Love, the Chairman of Texas Commerce, a bank that Chase absorbed on the way to becoming the second-largest bank in the US. Shipley says, "Tell is command and control. Sell is building consensus. Most people like to do something when they think it's their idea." As our profiled organizations demonstrate, committed cultures flourish in environments where leaders distribute control to the lowest levels of the organization and corporate success becomes "everyone's idea."
- **Keep it simple.** This advice does not imply that a culture of commitment is easy to build, or that its infrastructure will necessarily be simple. In fact, SAIC's employee-ownership policy requires a highly complex legal and financial structure. Yet at its heart, this strategy is simple: "Leadership, customers, and employees—as stakeholders, we're all in this together." To provide the compass that will guide their organizations through turbulent and confusing times, high-performing leaders rely on simple and clear value statements and unambiguous incentives.

A Parting Message: The Fundamental Things Apply

In the late 1990s, you could hardly pick up a book or magazine article about corporate culture without reading a glowing tale of Herman Miller, Inc., the office furniture manufacturer. Its now-retired CEO, Max DePree, even wrote a couple of best-selling books on culture. Ironically, just as the business press was touting the company's culture-centered approach to success, Herman Miller's expenses began to mount and it found itself barely able to break even. The Board of Directors quickly tapped Mike Volkema to be the new president of Herman Miller and lead a turnaround effort. His challenge: Get costs under control quickly in a venerable 75-year-old company that is an icon in the business literature.

To radically redesign a company that had been around for three-quarters of a century, Volkema decided to reconnect with the values that had originally made Herman Miller a success. He involved the entire management team, starting with front-line managers, in a discussion of corporate values and strategic direction. Out of these discussions grew Herman Miller's new manifesto of five core values. Boiled down, all five values reflect the importance of looking at business through the customer's perspective. To reconnect with customers, Herman Miller redesigned its production processes and revamped its corporate culture to create a rapid-response manufacturing environment. Two years later, it announced record sales, profits, and earnings per share. In the process of returning to its time-honored values, the organization found a way to meet the challenges of a new century filled with economic volatility.

As technology continues to drive the speed of business, leaders are constantly searching for new ways to serve customers and get ahead of the competition. High-performing leaders understand that while the lure of the new drives innovation, the wisdom of the old helps keep companies grounded in the fundamentals of success. As the leaders in this chapter demonstrate, none of these fundamentals is more important for holding a company together in turbulent times than a culture of commitment.

CHAPTER FOUR

PUT THE RIGHT PERSON IN THE RIGHT PLACE, RIGHT NOW

The best buy by way of management is brains—at any price.
—Malcolm Forbes

When you hire people who are smarter than you are,
you prove you are smarter than they are.
—R.H. Grant (with an obvious debt to Yogi Berra)

You think you're engaged in a war for talent where the stakes are high? Consider this: The fate of nations has rested on General Peter Schoomaker's hiring decisions.

As former Commander-in-Chief of the U.S. Special Operations Command, Schoomaker led the charge to reconfigure the government's most elite forces. Schoomaker, like most leaders today, understands the difficulty of hiring the right people to meet the challenges of a changing world. Since the end of the cold war, the Special Operations Forces (including the Delta Force, the Green Berets, the Army Rangers, the Navy Seals, and the Air Force Special Operations) have undergone a tremendous change in their mission, culture, and recruitment strategies. Schoomaker says, "There's a real blurring between the definitions of 'war' and 'peace,' 'domestic' and 'nondomestic,' 'economic' and 'military'. . . . SOF has always been mission focused. But now that mission has changed. We had to change along with it and develop new types of capabilities to fulfill it."

With the changes in the organization's mission have come changes in how commanders are selected and developed. Instead of looking for rough-and-ready "fighting machines," the SOF expects to find and train "warrior diplomats" and "quiet professionals." Schoomaker says, "You've got to select people with the highest likelihood of success. Then you have got to train, educate, and assess them constantly. You've got to keep upgrading the quality."

Because every SOF member must be able to serve as a leader, and Schoomaker believes that leadership means knowing how to deal with change, he doesn't have a cookie-cutter profile of the perfect SOF operative. Instead, he looks for people who display the behavioral, psychological, and intellectual qualities necessary for success. Schoomaker explains, "To make that assessment, we put people through a series of experiences in which they have to demonstrate whether they are capable of providing leadership. . . . For that reason we focus on teaching our people not just what to think but also how to think. . . . At the end of this process, a board of successful SOF members, led by a senior leader, decides who is in and who is not. The ultimate question board members ask is: "Do I want to serve and fight with this person at my side?"

As you prepare to face the challenges of a volatile and chaotic economy, look around and ask yourself: Do I have the right people fighting and serving at my side? Put another way, with everything that is facing our company/division/plant/etc., are the people we currently have in place the right people to move us forward? And, equally important, ask: What's the cost if these aren't the right people? In an upturn, the cost of not having the right people could be untold billions in lost and missed opportunities. In a downturn, the cost could be bankruptcy.

As you size up your most pressing challenges, you may find that you don't have the human resources to address them. New challenges demand new responses, and you may or may not be able to develop these solutions quickly with your current team. Remember what Einstein said: "We can't solve today's problems with yesterday's thinking." In other words, you may not have the right "thinkers"—the right people, in the right place, right now.

You're not alone if you don't have all the right people in place. Although it seems like it would be a top priority, the truth is that many leaders have not actively developed their ability to find and select the right people. Of course, the great business leaders have this ability, just like great sports coaches have it. But sadly, the sports examples are much more obvious than the business ones. Dean Smith, legendary basketball coach at North Carolina, selected Michael Jordan and James Worthy. Bela Karolyi, the larger-than-life gymnastics coach who's brought gymnasts to eight Olympics, selected Mary Lou Retton and Nadia Comaneci. In the business world, there are classic examples like Jack Welch, who selected so many extraordinary people that when he named Jeffrey Immelt as his successor, the two other executives under consideration for the job left the next day to head 3M and Home Depot. But move beyond Jack Welch and a handful of famous CEOs, and the list of great people selectors grows short very quickly.

Part of the disparity between the "right people" mindset in sports and business is due to the ease with which we can track the impact of individual talent in sports. But part of it also stems from business's lack of attention to the issue. Our research has found that only about 15 percent of companies actively differentiate between their high and low performers, and only 5 percent of companies actively select the high performers and remove the low performers. Most businesses are only now beginning to understand what sports has always understood: Having the right people does matter. Jerry Yang, co-founder of Yahoo!, puts it beautifully: "We value engineers like professional athletes. We value great people at 10 times an average person in their function."

To help you select the best people, we have provided a set of rules for putting the right people, in the right place, right now.

Rule 1: Know What You're Looking For

The first step is to define what you want "the right" people to do. This seems like a simple rule, but it is often forgotten in the rush to deal with pressing challenges. The "ready, fire, aim" school of management is as hazardous in hiring as it is anywhere else.

Before instituting a staffing change or addition, take the time to list your challenges and prioritize them in terms of immediacy and importance. Next, use this list of priorities to develop profiles of the people you will need. Only *after* you have defined the challenge and the skills you need to meet it can you begin to recruit candidates. In the words of the Red Queen in *Alice in Wonderland*, "If you don't know where you're going, any road will get you there."

In itself, simply scooping up talented people does not ensure success. (Of course, there are cases where a leader has hired a terrific person first and then created the job description later, but only rarely is this tactic successful.) Even the best people can fail if their talents are poorly matched to the job. For employees to be effective, they must work in a capacity that harnesses their strengths and meets the needs of the organization. Therefore, selection is as much about finding the right fit as it is finding the right person.

FedEx is one company that conscientiously considers goodness of fit in management development. As carefully as FedEx sorts packages, it sorts those with the drive and capacity for management from those who do not. "Most people don't realize all the rewards that management has to offer," says Bill Hooker, a senior human resources specialist at FedEx. "They also don't realize all the frustration." To help employees gauge their capacity for leadership, FedEx offers LEAP—the Leadership Evaluation and Awareness Process. LEAP began in the late 1980s once CEO Fred Smith realized that more than 10 percent of his first-time managers were leaving the company within fourteen months of taking on their management responsibilities. To reduce new manager attrition, the LEAP program begins with a full-day course called

"Is Management for Me?" The course provides employees with a realistic look at the challenges and rewards of leadership. As a result, fully 20 percent of the people who attend the course choose not to become leaders, opting for advancement via nonmanagement positions. This self-evaluation is just the first step in the series of rigorous evaluations that aspiring managers must undergo before they can complete the training process. In fact, only 20 percent of those who begin ever make it to the final step. Those who do, however, are undeniably qualified for the job.

As important as it is to develop accurate job profiles, it is equally important to share them with other leaders and gain consensus. If you believe the challenges to be of one type, but your colleagues —with whom your new hire will be working —have very different ideas, your new hire will be torn in different directions and most likely fail. (Note: Throughout the chapter, we refer to anyone filling a new role as a "new hire," whether he or she is a new recruit or has been with the organization for 20 years.) Therefore, high-performing leaders strongly recommend bringing the management team together to collaboratively develop a prioritized list of challenges and required skills for new positions.

Rule 2: Decide—In or Out?

In some cases, putting the right people in the right place means hiring outside talent to fill specially created roles. In other cases, it can simply mean reassigning your current staff to more appropriate positions. In still other situations, it can involve a combination of techniques; for example, creating a team to manage knowledge assets and then filling those roles with a mix of internal and external talent. Like any other staffing decision, the "in or out" question is a highly charged issue, particularly in times of volatility. The key to making a wise decision is to consider long-term benefit versus short-term costs.

Regrettably, in the midst of layoffs and hiring freezes, many firms will forego selecting the best people to minimize labor costs.

For example, in a recent engagement with a large manufacturing firm, we discovered that several crucial positions remained unfilled due to a hiring freeze. Even more troubling than the unfilled positions was the company's intention to limit their search to internal candidates—specifically, workers who had been targeted for layoffs. These were key positions, ones that could have had an impact on their slowing revenues. Rather than selecting the best candidates (whether internal or external), they were about to succumb to the path of least resistance. By contrast, leading companies will continue to select the best candidates in the midst of downsizing. Filling "play maker" roles with about-to-be-laid-off workers *simply because they're employees* is not usually in an organization's best interests, to say the least.

Of course, you can reap substantial benefits by hiring internal workers, including improved reputation (both within and outside the firm) and employee goodwill. But only if the fit is a good one. If an internal candidate is selected for a position where failure is very likely due to poor fit, then any benefits that would have been derived are not only cancelled, but criticism of leadership will be even more intense. Such moves inevitably lead to accusations of manipulation and poor planning, with some significant justification.

Rule 3: Look Behind the Résumé

In volatile times, leaders are often so desperate to make a hire that they fall into the trap of "selling" a position to a promising candidate. High-performing leaders, on the other hand, remember that they are buyers for the organization and its customers. Like every good shopper, they do a lot of comparative research before they plunk down their money.

When it comes time to evaluate candidates, you should conduct a thorough investigation of their capabilities vis-à-vis the open position. Unfortunately, many important skills do not show up on a résumé, nor are they easily quantifiable. Candidates don't usually walk through the door with a report card showing how well they can build a culture of commitment, deescalate anxiety, or harness knowledge assets. Technical skills, while important, are no substitute for the skills we've discussed in this book, which are essential for achieving success in volatile times.

High-performing leaders have developed two techniques for evaluating candidates: Work History Questioning and Continuum Reference Checking. Even if this is an internal hire, and even if it's someone with whom you've worked in the past, these techniques are critical for gaining an understanding of a candidate's ability to meet your current challenges.

Work History Questioning

During an interview, high-performing leaders focus on a candidate's work history, beginning with the first job and working toward the present in chronological order. The leader will also assess transitions —the reasons a candidate left one position for another.

Typically, the leader begins an interview by asking, "What is the first job you ever held?" It's important to note here that we're not talking about post-college jobs, but first-ever jobs. Whether that's a paper route, dishwasher, or lifeguard, as long as it's work related, the question, and the related experience, is fair game. The leader will then proceed by asking, "When did you leave? Why did you leave? What was the next position you held?" and so forth until the applicant's entire work history has been covered. This work-history review allows you to assess whether the applicant's experience is a good fit for the open position. And remember, experience in this context might mean a lot more than just industry experience or technical knowledge. It might mean dealing with difficult times, motivating others, building trust, etc. In addition, discussing the transitions from one job to another helps you understand what motivates and drives the candidate: pride, new challenges, money, recognition, excitement, etc.

This process is quite a bit different than the traditional "101 common interview questions" approach. The goal here is to dig deeper into the candidate's mind and get a feel for who he or she is and what he or she is about. The traditional approach usually generates a series of prepared answers, often in a disjointed order, and never really pierces the candidate's "interview veil." The work history approach, by contrast, takes you into the candidate's inner workings and helps to answer General Schoomaker's question: "Do I want to serve and fight with this person at my side?" The work-history approach provides the real-life flow of individual action that speaks concretely to a candidate's actual, not just intended, performance. It employs an interviewing technique similar to what clinical psychologists use and generates 30–50 percent more information than traditional interviews.

Continuum Reference Checking

Often thought of as a tedious formality, reference checking is actually one of the most critical aspects of selection. Reference checking serves a greater purpose than simply confirming academic credentials or résumé fact checking; it provides a glimpse into the skills and capabilities of candidates that don't appear on the résumé. We recommend a process called Continuum Reference Checking because it involves speaking with the full continuum of co-workers—colleagues, superiors, and even subordinates. Of course, they might not always give a complete picture of the candidate's skills and abilities, and it's unlikely that news will be wholly positive. In volatile times, leaders seek people who can make tough decisions, and tough decisions do not sit well with everyone. You may encounter people who do not particularly "like" a candidate, but like or dislike isn't really the issue. Rather, the question is whether the candidate can accomplish what you need him or she to accomplish. As advertising giant David Ogilvy said, "Our business needs a massive transfusion of talent. And talent, I believe, is most likely to be found among nonconformists, dissenters, and rebels."

Information drawn from references is a key predictor of what you'll see if and when the new hire joins your team. Larry Bossidy was Chairman and CEO of Allied Signal from 1991 to 1999, during which time he hired and promoted hundreds of leaders with a greater than 70-percent success rate. One of his most critical tools was Continùum Reference Checking. He advises:

> "It's essential to talk directly to references. When I arrived at Allied Signal, I personally checked references for dozens of candidates. I remember fellow CEOs asking: Why are you calling? I would answer that it was a personal concern of mine. If I'm going to hire someone, I don't want only human resources people checking them out; I want to check them out myself. And I don't talk to just one reference and leave the rest to human resources; I try to talk with two or three—even when it feels like there's absolutely no time to spare."

Of course, HR policies sometimes limit your abilitiy to gather information about a candidate. Nonetheless, a sufficiently diligent reference-checking process should enable you to make an informed decision. Had the Board of Coca-Cola used this technique with Douglas Ivester following legendary CEO Roberto Goizueta's untimely death, they might have spared themselves the erosion of millions in shareholder value. Prior to his succession to CEO at Coke, Ivester was CFO—and an excellent one, a number cruncher extraordinaire. And, since he had been Goizueta's second-in-command, the Board automatically gave him the job without checking with his colleagues. If only they had gone beyond the résumé, they would have found out that he lacked the visionary and interpersonal skills necessary for the CEO role.

One final caution: Beware of the candidate who is literally too good to be true. Often, you'll see candidates who have mastered the performance aspects of "job seeking," but fail in "job doing." This is one reason why we recommend Continuum Reference Checking; any questions about "job doing" should be answered during that process.

Rule 4: Look Beyond the Obvious

Sometimes the best candidate isn't the one right in front of you, waiting—or begging—to be picked. The right person for a job might work in another division of the organization—or even for a customer, supplier, or competitor. In other words, the "obvious" choice may not be the best one. Even when the best person for the job is obvious to a leader, it might not be to the candidate.

One of the pivotal events in the battle against Nazi Germany was the selection of Dwight David Eisenhower to lead Operation Overlord, the major Allied offensive designed to deliver the final coup de grace to Hitler's campaign in Europe. In making the decision to appoint Eisenhower, President Franklin Roosevelt and General George Marshall, Chief of Staff of the U.S. Armed Forces, changed the course of history.

George Marshall knew exactly what kind of person was needed—and it wasn't any of his most senior officers. Instead, Marshall needed someone driven by a higher motive; someone with the ability and strength to hold everyone accountable to the mission; someone both confident and humble enough to let others share the spotlight. "I knew that Eisenhower was the man," Marshall later said half-jokingly, "when I found out he was from Kansas." When Marshall finally asked Eisenhower how he would accomplish the Allies' objective, Eisenhower explained that for anyone but such charismatic geniuses as MacArthur and Patton (the "obvious" choices), the best route to success was *working through others.*

Hearing that, Marshall knew he had the right man. Eisenhower, on the other hand, wasn't quite so confident. He did accept the position, but only after more thought and discussion. And, of course, he did the job brilliantly and later went on to serve two terms as President of the United States.

The lesson of Eisenhower's story is that finding the right people takes both persistence and an open mind. Leaders must be unbiased as they define the position they want to fill, and then assertively seek out those with the best qualifications. Unfortunately, leaders frequently overlook the most qualified people because they develop job profiles that are too narrow or rooted in old biases. This is another reason why it is important to begin the job-description process with a definition of the challenge. If you assemble a profile of the perfect candidate based solely on technical skills, for example, you may miss the people with the leadership skills you really need. If IBM had taken such an approach and sought out a CEO with only extensive tech experience, they might have missed Lou Gerstner.

Rule 5: Get Comfortable with Discomfort

Because the "right people" aren't always obvious, you should take a closer look at people who might be qualified for a job—even if a first, superficial glance reveals that they don't meet your preconceived ideal. In this context, it's important to be aware of your own biases. Do you like a particular type of person? Do you have preconceptions about what kind of people will work hard and succeed? One of our clients employed an executive who would only hire people he found personally entertaining and humorous; if they seemed too serious, they didn't make the cut. Unfortunately, they all spent so much time laughing and enjoying each other's company that they were terribly unproductive, and ultimately unemployed.

Alternatively, when you open the hiring process to "uncomfortable" candidates, you can reap unforeseen benefits. In 1997, the T. J. Maxx chain was undergoing a growth spurt at the same time that the national unemployment rate was just 5 percent. They desperately needed warm bodies. So CEO Ben Cammerata publicly pledged to take 5,000 people off the welfare rolls by the year 2000. At that time, the welfare-to-work program was an experiment. Privately, Cammerata wondered if the new workers would be able to adjust to the workplace. He also wondered if they would cause morale problems with existing employees.

By the year 2000 T. J. Maxx had actually hired 16,000 people off welfare rolls instead of just 5,000. Sixty-one percent of the employees it hired through the welfare-to-work program were still employed one year later, well above the traditional 43-percent company retention rate for new hires. How did T. J. Maxx successfully recruit and retain so many workers? First, they kept an open mind about who the best people would be. In their case, desperation was the mother of invention. Once they had opened their minds to the possibility of hiring welfare workers, they hired a consulting agency to run a job hotline and helped train the welfare recipients. Although the job hotline brought in thousands of applicants, T. J. Maxx still had one important problem: Many of these applicants were unprepared for the world of work. To help them adjust to employment, T. J. Maxx started a pilot program that gave welfare recipients classroom training, followed by an internship. The program also provided customized assistance in the areas of childcare and transportation. Explains one store manager, "The job market is such that you can't always hire good people—you have to make them."

Rule 6: Let Them Do Their Job

As T. J. Maxx illustrates, even finding the right people and putting them in the right place may not be enough to ensure success. You also need to provide the right environment for achievement. Some people may need a little extra help. Others, particularly the highly talented and qualified, might just need to be pointed in the right direction and then turned loose. Once you've hired the right people, trust that you've done your job and let them do theirs. Make sure they have the resources, support, and flexibility to accomplish what they've been asked to do, and then let them do it.

Perhaps no situation better exemplifies the dangers of fencing in employees than recent troubles at Xerox. In the late 1990s, Xerox was riding the wave of Wall Street infatuation with tech stocks. In May 1999, just three weeks after G. Richard (Rick) Thoman replaced Paul Allaire as CEO, Xerox hit a record high of nearly $64 a share. Then, in the third quarter of 1999, Xerox confounded predictions by posting an 11-percent drop in income. Investors quickly deserted Xerox, cutting nearly 25 percent of its value in a single day.

These financial problems exacerbated the existing tensions between Thoman and other Xerox executives. As with most other break-ups, their relationship had started well. Allaire, who moved into the role of Chairman when he hired Thoman—and who ultimately fired Thoman—said, "We were looking for a change agent, and he seemed to be a perfect match." Unfortunately, Thoman was never able to get Xerox to do more than talk about change, despite a sterling reputation, several advanced degrees, and a career spent as second-in-command to Louis V. Gerstner at McKinsey, AmEx, and IBM. Thoman took the job at Xerox as an opportunity to shine on his own as CEO of a major corporation. That chance never really unfolded.

Thoman insists that he never had the authority he needed to be an effective leader. He alleges that Xerox's board, led by Allaire, prevented him from developing his own management team. "The analogy to my experience would have been if Lou Gerstner had tried to turn around IBM with John Akers still there—and without his own team," he says. In retrospect, Thoman says he should have insisted that Allaire step down as chairman after transferring his CEO title. Of course, Allaire never directly told Thoman what to do or blatantly undermined his authority. Although Allaire never spoke up at management meetings, he undermined his successor by his mere presence. Says one former top executive: "I knew it was doomed to fail when Rick and Paul would be in the same meeting and the line of eyes around the table would keep focusing on Paul even though Rick was doing all the talking."

While outsiders like Thoman face special challenges in new roles, internal candidates have to walk through equally dangerous minefields. With internal promotions, performance problems can occur when leaders do not free new hires from their previous duties so they can succeed in their new duties. Rather than officially leaving one position for another, people end up taking on a second job. In the long term, this is an untenable solution. In healthcare, for example, when staff nurses are promoted to nurse managers, they often keep doing their staff-nursing duties. In fact, the average nurse manager spends less than 25 percent of his or her time on management work while retaining 100 percent of the management accountability. Not only is this stressful situation avoidable, it also helps explain why jobs in management are often viewed as undesirable. If your managers are only managing 25 percent of the time, they won't have time to prevent teamwork, productivity, and communication problems—much less deal with them when they inevitably crop up.

Case Studies: Bringing the Rules to Life

You've probably heard about the organizations in these two case studies: Home Depot and the U.S. Olympic Committee. What you might not know are the creative ways they have found to put the right people in the right place using the rules we just discussed. As you review the case studies, notice how each organization found rational ways to manage putting the right people in the right places—a process that is too often irrational in volatile times.

Home Depot: Automating the HR Process

Standard business wisdom says that hiring and promoting are people-intensive activities. Managers must meet with candidates to test their skills, judge their character, and measure their goodness of fit with the organization and the position. This piece of wisdom is true—to a point. The fallacy lies in thinking that because the ultimate hiring decision is human-intensive, the entire process needs to be. Unfortunately, all the people involved in the process bring their unconscious biases to it. Despite well-intentioned efforts to embrace diversity, most people unwittingly revert to hiring people who are like themselves. As a result, organizations inadvertently weed out many highly qualified candidates, thus losing the potential for quality and innovation they represent.

Alan Frost at Home Depot looked at the problem from another angle: What if organizations could take the subjectivity out of the hiring process by automating a portion of it? But Frost's suggestion was not a result of altruism, as you might think. Rather, it was a response to a very real economic threat.

In 1998, a group of women threatened Home Depot with a $135-million class-action lawsuit, charging that women were steered to low-paying positions and passed over for promotion. At the same time the hardware retail behemoth was beginning to face market saturation, they now faced another economic danger: the immediate costs of the lawsuit and the potential follow-up costs of a boycott by women and minority consumers. Home Depot settled the lawsuit quickly, stipulating that every qualified applicant would have the opportunity for the position of his or her choice. Enter Alan Frost and his JPP (Job Preference Program).

In the new system, both new applicants and employees seeking a promotion answer a brief career questionnaire via in-store kiosks or an 800-number. The computer system matches their skills and experience to open positions, and then sends their employment application to every store within a commutable radius. In fact, if an employee applies for a position for which he or she is unqualified, the system generates a customized career plan for the employee, showing which skills they need to develop and which positions are prerequisites for their desired job.

To date, the system has been a huge success at improving diversity. The numbers of female managers have increased by 30 percent and minority managers by 28 percent. Home Depot has seen an 11-percent decrease in turnover, a significant problem for retail operations.

In addition to these expected benefits, the system has generated some other surprising results. Morale in the management ranks has improved now that the new system weeds out unqualified candidates so managers don't have to. JPP also broadens the pool of applicants by sending store managers the profiles of every viable candidate within driving distance.

Applicants and employees are happier, too, because the system eliminates some of their own biases that restrict their career opportunities. Take the case of Claudia Corral. Although she had spent most of her life working with an uncle in his contracting business, when she went to apply for a job at her local Home Depot, she listed "cashier" as her desired position. "That's where I thought women went," Claudia shrugs. However, the computer matched her as a candidate for sales associate in building materials, which paved the way for a career in management.

Although their initial motivation came from a lawsuit, Home Depot quickly realized the advantage of going beyond their preconceived ideas about candidates to find the right people and put them in the right place. By automating the screening process, Home Depot was able to eliminate the barriers of subjectivity in "knowing what to look for" and "going beyond the résumé." Although JPP may have been uncomfortable for some, at least at the beginning, "getting comfortable with discomfort" gave Home Depot the competitive advantage of diversity and strengthened its relationships with employees and customers.

The U.S. Olympic Committee: Bearing the Torch

Swifter. Higher. Stronger. The English translation of the official Olympic motto describes the qualities that every person or organization needs to triumph over the competition. When it comes to putting the right people in the right place, the U.S. Olympic Committee lives up to its motto.

The USOC supports more than 25,000 aspiring Olympic athletes each year, providing three state-of-the-art training facilities, grants for athletes, and preparation and coordination for eight major competitions. With just 450 employees and a $125-million annual budget, the USOC clearly knows how to get the most out of its staff. All of this success comes despite the fact that the USOC pays less for the same position than for-profit businesses can. Even more remarkable is the organization's turnover rate of just 5 percent. The tenure of the average manager at the USOC is more than seven years, and 8 percent of employees have been there for more than ten years.

The USOC attributes its success to developing and living an inspiring vision. Of course, helping athletes make it to the Olympics is the kind of vision that attracts and inspires employees, low salaries notwithstanding—and everywhere they turn, employees are reminded of that vision. The campus is filled with Olympic-themed art, from statues in courtyards to posters on the walls to the T-shirts that many staffers wear. It also helps that staffers are close to their work, with daily contact with athletes in training. "Every day, we see the direct impact of our work," explains Darryl Seibel, director of media and public relations. "It makes you feel good to drive into the parking lot and see the boxing team out for a run."

Because staffing an Olympic event is a logistical nightmare that literally takes years to plan, the USOC has developed an algorithm for staffing. "Knowing how many staff members we can afford to send makes it easier for us to plan and negotiate our staffing needs with the national governing bodies," explains Greg Harney, managing director of games and organizational support.

After the planning comes the actual competition, an event that requires hundreds of additional temporary staff. Rather than use temporary agencies, the USOC has found creative ways to staff up for the event. "We don't really hire anyone specifically for the event," Harney explains. In addition to sending permanent employees in the International Games Division who are experts at the games, the USOC "borrows" employees from other areas of the organization and external sponsors. The trick to borrowing employees, Harney says, is maintaining good relationships with the organizations that may have to do without key staff members for the duration of the event.

In times of intense activity, jobs get changed as well as added. When a major event like the Summer Olympics or Pan American Games comes along, employees who staff the events can easily put in lots of overtime in areas unrelated to the typical work assignments. To ease the transition between the normal routine and the "big event," the USOC creates event-specific job descriptions for all employees, detailing their temporary duties and reporting requirements.

Because the job is so flexible and challenging, the USOC needs to hire the right people. It does so by hiring good customer partners—and good customers. In order to better understand and serve its customers—the athletes it supports— the USOC recruits people who pursue the values of the Olympics in their personal and professional lives. It also hires former customers to serve as spokespeople for the company. The USOC's PR director is Benita Fitzgerald Mosely, a former track-and-field Olympian who was a gold medalist in the 100-meter hurdles in the 1980s. "I'm ideally suited to this job," she says. "I have a passion for athletics and in one way or another I've been affiliated with the USOC all of my life. I think it's important for employers to hire people with a passion for what they do. This ensures these folks will give their all in their jobs."

As an organization whose very existence is defined by volatile swings in staffing needs, the USOC offers important lessons for any leader trying to manage in turbulent times. Many of their solutions, like the "beg, borrow, or steal" temporary staffing method, are creative ways to go beyond the obvious. Another core element of their success is their ability to inspire employees to "give their all" by driving their values through the entire HR process—from recruitment to job descriptions to staffing plans and training. Like many other high-performing organizations, the USOC simplifies these processes by tapping into those who share its values. This values-driven approach is anything but soft, however, as the USOC uses hard data to find the right people in the right numbers and put them in the right place.

Practical Strategies for Putting the Right People in the Right Place, Right Now

- **In God we trust; all others must use data.** No one is saying that instinct doesn't have a part in the hiring process. Sometimes you play a hunch and it works out wonderfully; at other times, you get bad "vibes" about someone that later turn out to be justified. However, it's much more common for a leader to hire a candidate based on personal comfort, only to find that the best interests of the organization weren't served. Like Home Depot, you can minimize subjectivity and balance it as much as possible with objective criteria. Define what the role needs to do, and then assess the candidate's goodness of fit for that role using measurable and consistent criteria.

- **Don't go it alone.** Headhunters, employment agencies, and the classified ads all can be useful in gathering information and rooting out candidates. Unfortunately, these forums can be expensive and produce spotty results. However, that doesn't mean you can't rely on a network of people to help bring candidates to your attention. Also, use customers, suppliers, references from current employees—even competitors—to identify the best candidates. Once they come to your door, though, it is your responsibility to put the right people in the right place.
- **Project staffing needs.** Employees are important assets that generate revenue. Why not treat your human resource needs with the same level of planning and foresight as your financial projections? High-performing companies take the time to assess their situation and project future needs, even in volatile times. Recruitment is one area where it is vitally important to make haste slowly. If you constantly monitor the need for staff, and continuously troll the waters for the best people, you won't need to make hasty—and costly—decisions.

A Parting Message: Know When to Delegate

Leaders put a lot of effort into getting the right person into the right place. Once they accomplish that task, their next one is—

paradoxically—to let go. While hiring cannot be delegated, the work for which one hires must be. In volatile times, leaders must put the right people in the right place to free *themselves* to be in the right place.

Timothy Firnstahl, CEO of Restaurant Service, Inc., learned this lesson as his company grew beyond his ability to hold the helm alone. In 1983, Firnstahl's business had grown to include three restaurants, a service company, and a wholesale fish seller, collectively bringing in $10 million in annual sales. Putting in seven-day weeks was no longer an option, so Firnstahl decided to expand his management team. In the process, he discovered four "personal" problems that, in fact, every leader encounters when trying to put the right people in the right place. As he recalls:

> "The first and most obvious problem was watching someone mess up a task I could do easily in half the time. I had to learn to keep my mouth shut since interceding would frustrate my new subordinate, not to mention use up the time I wanted to save. The second problem had to do with identity, specifically mine. . . . I had to give up the particular skills for which I was known and the gratification that went with applying them. Third was the problem of competitiveness. . . . I had to watch while others reached ability levels superior to my own. . . . Finally there was the problem of leasrning a whole new job. Now I had to decide where the company should go. . . . and keep the company on track. Learning this new job meant leaving my comfort zone for the unknown. It meant learning the art of leadership."

CHAPTER FIVE

MAXIMIZE KNOWLEDGE ASSETS

We did not get the intelligence information needed to predict that this was about to happen, to be aware of this kind of event coming our way.

—Secretary of State Colin Powell

On September 11, 2001, perhaps the greatest knowledge-management failure in history occurred. The Central Intelligence Agency, the State Department's visa screening, the Federal Bureau of Investigation, the Immigration and Naturalization Service's domestic security, and the Federal Aviation Administration's airport security all failed to identify, store, access, create, and share the knowledge assets necessary to prevent the worst terrorist attack in American history.

It would take an entire book to list all of the knowledge-management breakdowns that have occurred within and between these agencies with respect to terrorist threats, but here are two. Over the past two years, the CIA made the FBI aware of the names of numerous suspected members of Osama bin Laden's terrorist network thought to be headed to, or already in, the United States. The FBI sent the names to INS, but by the time any actions were taken, most of the suspected terrorists were already hiding in the U.S. Two of the names specifically referenced were aboard the hijacked airplane that crashed into the Pentagon. Prior to the 1993 World Trade Center bombing, a suspected terrorist was arrested in New York in possession of numerous files from his terror organization that weren't immediately translated because the local FBI office couldn't procure a translator. When they were finally translated, it was so poorly done that the name of Al Qaeda was mistranslated. The suspect was later linked to those who committed the 1993 bombing.

If September 11 made one point crystal clear, it's that maximizing your knowledge assets is essential to protecting against chaos and uncertainty. As Colin Powell emphasized, we need to be able to predict what's about to happen, what's coming our way. While this is glaringly obvious in matters of national security, it is equally critical for the survival and progress of business and the economy. To the extent that business leaders can mine the knowledge assets of their people, they have anticipatory power—they can more accurately see the future. And if they can see the future, they can prepare for, and even avoid, the danger inherent in economic volatility.

Truth be known, the economic volatility that most businesses feel is driven largely by ignorance—ignorance as to customer preferences, demand shifts, suppliers' future plans, competitors' new offerings, technological breakthroughs, and so on. Thus, to the extent that you can increase your corporate intelligence—by identifying, harnessing, storing, accessing, creating, and sharing knowledge assets—you can provide protection against volatility.

Knowledge Assets

An organization's ability to harness and maximize knowledge assets in the twenty-first century plays a dominant role in creating competitive advantage. More than financial or physical assets, knowledge assets are increasingly becoming the raw material of work and the main driver of business success. In a volatile and chaotic economy, it's easy to set aside knowledge management to focus on short-term measures like cost cutting. Yet managing knowledge assets is so important that it's one of only three processes for which GE's former CEO Jack Welch, the Manager of the Century himself, took personal responsibility.

What are knowledge assets? Simply put, knowledge assets are everything that everyone in your organization knows. They include skills; experience; relationships with clients or vendors; patents; trademarks; competitive insight; procedures; marketing strategies; the knowledge contained in every fax; e-mail, and document; and more.

Debate is growing about the ability of current accounting systems to accurately measure these most important corporate assets. In January 2000, Alan Greenspan noted that accounting measures were not accurately reflecting investments in knowledge assets and warned of future problems because of this deficiency. Groups of prominent accountants have started to develop measures to track knowledge assets more accurately in order to reflect the true value of a company.

Baruch Lev, an accounting professor at NYU, has developed a financial measure he calls Knowledge Capital Earnings (KCE). This measure, which tracks the contribution of intangible (e.g., knowledge) assets to earnings, is making an impressive showing in early test runs. In a recent study that pitted cash flow, traditional earnings, and KCE against one another to statistically predict returns on a company's stock, Lev found KCE to be the clear winner. This research confirmed what high-performing leaders already know: Knowledge assets are a major source of competitive advantage, and companies with the greater returns on knowledge assets see greater financial returns. To maximize their knowledge assets, benchmark leaders follow five rules of knowledge management.

Rule 1: Take Stock of Current Knowledge Assets

Measuring financial capital is fairly straightforward. Barring illegal activity, most organizations can easily measure the balances in their various accounts. The same holds true for physical capital. While it may be cumbersome to measure inventory across divisions or facilities, experienced auditors can accomplish the task easily and accurately.

Unfortunately, the same is not always true of knowledge assets. When knowledge assets are in an explicit form, e.g., software, patents, training materials, etc., you can readily identify and catalog them. However, the vast majority of knowledge assets are tacit rather than explicit. This means they exist in the skills, experience, relationships, and insights of employees, which makes them difficult to quantify.

As difficult as that task is, however, it is absolutely necessary. Every bit of intellectual capital that isn't tracked and measured could be costing your organization millions of dollars in lost opportunities. Most executives would never leave a million dollars in cash sitting in a box in the CFO's office because of the lost investment returns—yet a great many don't give a second thought to the lost gains from ignored knowledge assets. And particularly in a tight economy, squeezing every drop of return from every asset you own is critical. The following are a few examples of the forms that these "opportunity costs" can take.

Lost Revenue

Many organizations lose potential revenue through "lost innovation"—the inability to bring good ideas to market. The problem is not that creative ideas don't exist within organizations; rather, it is that they lie untapped. Without systems for identifying and promoting them, these untapped ideas either die or go elsewhere. We may never know how many great ideas have been lost in this way. However, we can assume that the increase in technology startups in the past five to ten years has been at least partially driven by frustrated inventors leaving their established organizations to develop their ideas on their own terms.

Lost Customers

Closely tied to the lost revenue issue, customer loss occurs when organizations fail to make customer partnerships or share the information gleaned from them. When organizations restrict access to customer information, they lose critical knowledge that could help operations, R&D, and finance in developing products and services. For example, how many product launches have failed, only to have people from marketing or sales say "I could have told you that would happen, but you didn't ask"? Because of this lack of communication, organizations lose credibility with existing customers and have difficulty attracting new ones.

Lost Profit

Perhaps the most common lost opportunity occurs with not amassing knowledge assets that offer increased efficiencies or cost savings. GE's famous Work-Out program was designed specifically to gather ideas for efficiency and cost savings directly from front-line employees.

While GE worked through group sessions and town hall meetings, other firms have adopted various technologies to take stock of their knowledge assets. In fact, most organizations pursuing knowledge management today do so from an IT perspective. However, technology is only one of the two major components of a knowledge-management system. The other is people.

The information that emerges from a knowledge-management system is only as complete and reliable as that which goes into it. Before an organization can centralize knowledge in a software system, it must first elicit that knowledge from its people. So before you start shopping for relational databases or hiring XML programmers, you should engage your staff in developing an inventory of knowledge assets. The method of engagement will differ depending on your organization and industry—writing case studies and articles, developing educational/training materials, Internet/Intranet discussion/chat areas, or formal/informal discussion forums. Just as with customer partnerships, cataloging knowledge assets should involve all areas and levels of the organization.

For example, Ritz-Carlton enriches its knowledge-management system from a collection of index cards compiled by associates. Each time an associate has a customer encounter, he or she notes the customer's preferences. Then this information is entered into a database and called up the next time a guest registers at another Ritz-Carlton hotel.

Rule 2: Mobilize the Intellectual Capital You Already Have

Once you have identified your knowledge assets base, the next step is to find a mechanism for integrating and sharing that knowledge across the organization. Just as you gather knowledge assets from every corner of the organization, you must also disseminate those assets back through the same channels. Sharing information ensures that each person can harness the knowledge of the whole—and vice versa—to improve customer service, increase profits, and enhance competitive position.

On an *intraorganizational* basis, knowledge dissemination often involves the creation of an intellectual capital "library," with access via Internet/Intranet, electronic or physical discussion spaces, educational offerings and training, meetings, videoconferences, and other formal/informal sharing forums. Dow Chemical has been extremely successful with this method of maximizing knowledge assets. Since it has entered all 2,000. of its patents in a central database, all divisions can now search the system to find new applications for existing products. The result? New sources of revenue with no new R&D expense. Especially in a turbulent economy, that's something every CEO can support.

Successful leaders also disseminate knowledge on an *interorganizational* basis. In today's networked business environment, it is equally important to share knowledge with other organizations, including strategic partners, allies, intermediaries, and suppliers. For example, Boeing engages customers and suppliers in "paperless" development of aircraft using an integrated digital database. Like Boeing, when you get business partners tapped into your knowledge processes, you're better able to align strategies and goals, and create efficiencies.

Rule 3: Create New Intellectual Capital

The way to maintain your organization's competitive advantage over the long term is not just to harness existing knowledge assets, but to develop new ones. The first step in this process is to conduct a "gap analysis" between current and ideal knowledge assets. First, assess your competitive landscape—including customers, competitors, potential competitors, partners, etc.—to identify your organization's strategic direction and specific objectives. Next, compare these objectives to the current knowledge assets available to fulfill them. This analysis will help you see if and where your knowledge assets are too low (i.e., high-return opportunities are available if you had the necessary capital), or adequate (i.e., the costs of creating new knowledge assets outweighs the likely benefits). Third, identify potential sources of any missing knowledge assets. Ask whether your organization has the internal capacity to develop these assets cost-effectively, or would it be better to acquire the capability from an external expert.

For example, when a firm like Cisco evaluates potential acquisitions, they consider the extent to which the potential acquiree offers knowledge assets in a necessary area. If Cisco identifies a market opportunity for which they don't currently have sufficient knowledge assets, they will look for acquisition targets that fulfill that need. If a potential acquisition target offers knowledge assets in areas where Cisco is already strong, they will likely pass on the deal. Just as with most forms of capital, knowledge assets have diminishing returns, so it's important to invest wisely.

When you do create new intellectual capital, you'll find that growth in knowledge assets is exponential, not linear. Each new piece of capital is likely to generate a "synergistic kick"—an exponential explosion—of knowledge assets and value creation. This explosion of new knowledge helps position the organization for increased dominance in current markets, entry into as-yet-undiscovered markets and other profit-generating opportunities.

Particularly in volatile times, a key risk that organizations must acknowledge is underinvestment in knowledge assets. In a knowledge-driven economy, knowledge assets represent revenue and profits. Without these assets, there's simply nothing to sell or generate profit. Tom Davenport, a business professor at Boston University, has observed that harnessing and creating knowledge assets is a ceaseless process. But he has a tough question for executives who'd rather avoid the effort: "How much does it cost an organization to forget what key employees know, to be unable to answer customer questions quickly or at all, to make poor decisions based on faulty knowledge, or miss key business opportunities?" It's important to remember that harnessing and creating knowledge assets represent a solution to, and not a cause of, turbulent times.

Rule 4: Build a Knowledge Balance Sheet

How do you measure the real benefit from finding, harnessing, and creating knowledge assets? After all, we said earlier that traditional accounting systems have not yet begun to capture knowledge assets. Consider this question from Australian business professor Karl-Erik Sveiby: "How do your accountants . . . treat the costs for your trip to meet and build relationships with the new staff in a recently acquired subsidiary? As a cost! How do these same accountants treat the extension of your firm's fiber optics cable network to the new office? As an investment!"

Sveiby hails from Sweden, a country where he pioneered knowledge management, and where companies such as Skandia and Telia, Sweden's major telecom company, now publish annual reports listing their human resources and intellectual capital. Some companies have even gone so far as to replace traditional financial statements with knowledge-assets statements.

In this chapter, we are not going to argue for the wholesale revision of accounting and financial statements. We are going to suggest, however, a model for thinking about knowledge assets called a Knowledge Balance Sheet.

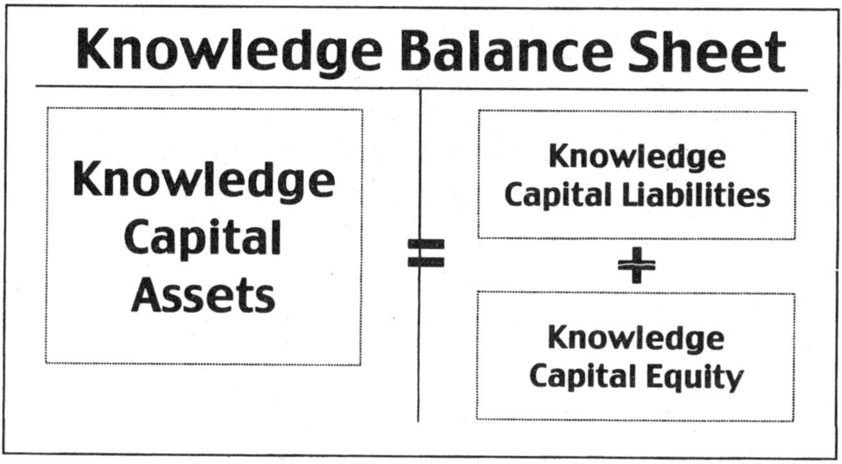

Like the similarly-named financial balance sheet, the Knowledge Balance Sheet tracks a company's assets and their sources. Also like the traditional balance sheet, Knowledge Capital Assets equals the sum of Knowledge Capital Liabilities and Knowledge Capital Equity. The Knowledge Balance Sheet points out that Knowledge Assets can come from within the organization (e.g., the skills, talents, insights, and relationships of current employees) or from outside the organization (e.g., strategic alliances, license agreements, acquisitions, etc.).

For example, if a consulting firm wants to increase its knowledge assets in an area like benchmarking, it could build a best-practices benchmarking database by purchasing the appropriate programming technology and gathering the relevant data (a.k.a. equity) or by purchasing a license for data-usage rights and fully-developed software from a benchmarking company (a.k.a. liabilities). Or, if a manufacturer needs greater knowledge assets in the area of process improvements, it may opt to hire several process engineers (equity) or hire a consulting firm (liabilities). In both of these examples, the firm is generating returns on the assets being used. In either case, the size of the Knowledge Asset base grows in proportion to the size of Knowledge Asset Liabilities and Knowledge Asset Equity.

Rule 5: Create a Knowledge-Sharing Culture

We once had a client who tried to restrict the flow of information across the organization because he personally wanted to be able to authenticate and verify all of the information before staff used it to make decisions. Of course, by the time he authenticated the data, the opportunity to make an important decision had long passed.

The traditional command-and-control, hierarchical view of the organization often impedes efforts to harness a company's knowledge assets. Even in flatter, more fluid organizations, you can still find cultural or structural barriers to the flow of information. High-performing leaders overcome these barriers by building cultures that actively encourage knowledge sharing and creation. To do so, they follow these guidelines:

- Identify and eradicate organizational practices and incentives that promote knowledge hoarding and punish knowledge sharing.
- Involve all areas of the organization (including executive leadership, front-line management, HR, finance, etc.) in developing a culture that rewards knowledge sharing. This might mean developing new incentive systems or reconfiguring the organization's architecture. Some organizations, like Texas Instruments, offer tangible rewards for contributing to their knowledge assets. Other companies, like consulting firms, make knowledge asset contributions an explicit and essential component of every job role.
- Integrate with the core business. While some organizations prefer to consolidate the management of knowledge assets in a single person's role, we have found it more effective to distribute knowledge management across the organization. You

can accomplish this distribution via integration into job descriptions, performance appraisals, and mission statements. So many change initiatives fail to deliver results because they are special projects that remain sectioned off from the rest of the organization. When any effort is not integrated with the organization's core daily life, employees see it as just another "flavor of the month" and hope it disappears. Harnessing the organization's most important assets should not fall into this trap.

- Teach people how to share information. Leaders need to provide tools to capture and harness the firm's knowledge assets. These tools may be simple guides to help people navigate the process of providing information, or they may be complex relational databases on Intranets with video-conferencing. For example, Matsushita in Japan and Ikea in Sweden use simulations to orient new hires and managers to their knowledge-management processes. Form follows function in this respect, and the tools you choose should be a function of people's technological sophistication, comfort, cost, business needs, and expected implementation success.

Like all cultural changes, a culture of knowledge management only works if it gains acceptance both horizontally and vertically throughout the organization. Internal champions who can procure the necessary resources, support, and enthusiasm are essential. However, knowledge-management projects with only one strong supporter or champion tend to fail. We have found that most successful knowledge-management efforts have used more than one supporter to really get the ball rolling.

Finally, it is not enough for employees to start using a knowledge-management system; they need to keep using the system. You can acquire initial users by establishing policies and promotional systems, but you can only *keep* users by designing a culture that rewards the sharing and creation of knowledge. The case studies in the next section illustrate how benchmark leaders make knowledge management a central part of their organization's culture.

Case Studies: Bringing the Rules to Life

In this section we provide two case studies that illustrate two different, yet successful approaches. The first case study shows how harnessing knowledge assets can help improve sales and staff retention, particularly in a volatile economy. The second case study shows how investment in knowledge assets can help deal with the most volatile situation of them all: a heart attack. Both case studies illustrate that knowledge assets—wherever and however they are gained—provide strong competitive advantage.

Frito-Lay: Harnessing Knowledge to Increase Sales

Frito-Lay executives saw a growing problem in 1999 that no leader wants to have during times of economic uncertainty—declining morale and productivity of the sales team. Salespeople, who were scattered across ten different cities, complained about geographic isolation and disconnection from the rest of the team. With no central repository of corporate information, salespeople would ask the corporate support staff for the same types of information, forcing them to perform the same tasks over and over. Turnover increased as salespeople quit over the difficulty of finding vital information and communicating it to the rest of the team.

"We had knowledge trapped in files everywhere," explains Mike Marino, Vice President of Customer Development at Frito-Lay. The problem: No one knew how to tap it. Marino and his team knew that if the 15-member sales team could only access the same information in one central location, they would experience fewer frustrations with information sharing and communication. They also knew that an online capacity for brainstorming and collaboration would help salespeople overcome their feelings of isolation.

Marino's group realized there was one solution to these disparate challenges—a knowledge-management portal on the corporate Intranet. Such a system would provide a central location for all customer information and streamline information sharing. In addition to up-to-the minute information about the team's customers, the portal would house profiles on key people throughout

Frito-Lay, so salespeople could find expert advisors and collaborators at the click of a mouse.

The portal went live in January 2000, and since then three additional sales teams have gone online. In its first year of implementation, the system has delivered positive results in three critical operational areas.

First, the system has streamlined the flow of information. The pilot group can share documents concurrently online instead of sending multiple faxes across the country. "We have to manipulate large amounts of data, and now we can look at it online versus having to have somebody physically travel to the retail customer. It's almost a distance learning tool as much as anything else," says Joe Ackerman, a customer team leader in the sales division based in Portland, Oregon.

Second, the system has generated revenue. "What we expected to see was that the pilot team would outperform others in terms of sales and profitability," Marino says. And, in fact, the test team doubled the growth rate of its main customer's business in the salty snack category. "The retailer is happy because they're doing more business in their market, and we're doing business at a faster growth rate with this customer than with other customers," Marino explains.

Third, the knowledge-management portal has boosted morale and retention. Since the portal has been in place, not one person on the original 15-member team has left. Ackerman attributes this directly to the portal, "because it helps build the connection." In fact, the pilot portal was so successful that it is being used at PepsiCo, Frito-Lay's parent company. With new added functions, employees across all PepsiCo can share and maximize knowledge about jointly shared customers.

St. Joseph's Hospital: Putting Knowledge at Doctors' Fingertips

Imagine that you come to the emergency room of St. Joseph's Hospital in Phoenix complaining of chest pain. After the doctor does a physical assessment of your condition, she pulls out her palmtop computer and starts clicking away. Is she checking her e-mail or stock quotes at a time like this? No. Your doctor is logging into St. Joseph's Webbased MI (myocardial infarction) diagnostic protocol. After asking you a few questions from the protocol, your doctor determines that you have indigestion and sends you home with a couple of antacids. But another patient suffering from similar symptoms—someone actually having a heart attack—is caught by the protocol and routed for immediate lifesaving treatment.

St. Joseph's high-tech diagnostic brings the standards of best practice to the high-touch, but often subjective and unreliable task of diagnosis. "Every physician's experience can be colored by the unique characteristics of the particular patients that they have cared for," says Dr. Philip Fracica, medical director of the ICU and other pulmonary and cardiac units at St. Joseph's. "But are those experiences truly representative of all patients?"

Without the handheld system, doctors would be hard-pressed to tell. With new clinical studies coming out almost every day, doctors find it nearly impossible to remember every pertinent finding. And in heart attack assessment, which requires quick decision-making, trying to recall last month's article in the *New England Journal of Medicine* can waste precious minutes. Of course, one can't always assume that doctors are familiar with new treatment protocols, since many doctors are too busy to keep current with the medical literature.

So when he learned about an objective scoring system for assessing heart attack risk at one of the hospital's monthly educational sessions, Dr. Fracica decided to implement it. Dr. Fracica called in a California-based software developer that specializes in delivering enterprise applications to handheld computers. While assessing a patient, ER doctors can follow a link on their PDAs' browser to a Web page on St. Joseph's server that contains the risk-assessment evaluation. The software enables the Web page to transfer the information literally to the doctors' fingertips. The Web pages are then stored on the users' PDAs, until doctors decide to delete them. This way, doctors can access the Web pages on subsequent occasions without having to download them again, which saves even more precious minutes. At the end of the assessment, the program returns the heart attack risk for a specific patient, and the doctor can treat accordingly.

All 14 of St. Joseph's emergency room physicians have been using the application since June of 2000. While no one can quantify exactly how many additional lives have been saved or put a value on those lives, doctors at St. Joseph's are making more informed decisions more quickly. This would be a great achievement in a traditional business setting (how many e-commerce companies failed to deliver on promises of *more information more quickly*?). But in an environment where the effects of volatility go way beyond a loss on an income statement, harnessing knowledge assets can literally mean the difference between life and death.

Practical Strategies for Maximizing Knowledge Assets

At first glance, these two organizations appear to have taken two different approaches to knowledge management. Nevertheless, regardless of whether they looked inside or outside for knowledge solutions, they both followed some basic strategies to strengthen their Knowledge Balance Sheet:

- **Integrate tacit and explicit knowledge.** As our case studies illustrate, successful knowledge-management systems maximize their investments in objects *and* processes, technology *and* people. Successful leaders harness knowledge assets by engaging people to gather knowledge in all its forms, and then using technology to share that knowledge and create exponential growth.
- **Provide continuous support.** All organizations manage knowledge in informal ways, from water-cooler discussions to catch-as-catch-can efforts to update corporate materials.

Only formal efforts, however, provide the sustained and centralized system that can harness an entire organization's knowledge assets. To sustain a formal system, leaders must integrate it into the culture and continually champion and encourage system usage.

- **Be pragmatic.** While Frito-Lay tapped its internal experts, St. Joseph's Hospital realized that it needed a knowledge infusion from outside of the organization and its medical staff. The Knowledge Balance Sheet reinforces the notion that both strategies contribute to the total knowledge assets of the organization. The pivotal question is: Where are your organization's knowledge gaps, and who or what can fill them?

A Parting Message: What You Measure Is What You Value

We made this point in Chapter 3 on culture, but it bears repeating here. When we look at our profiled leaders, we see that they're just a little bit ahead of their time. In the old economy, companies tracked financial and material assets while discounting people as expenses. Today, we value employees as knowledge workers in a knowledge economy. Not only do high-performing leaders recognize this fact, they also measure what they value.

One example of this forward-thinking leadership is the Department of Defense. In the past, nothing epitomized "command and control" more than the military, and perhaps no individual was considered as dispensable as a foot soldier. Yet today, military leaders are pushing knowledge out to the individual soldier, tracking and sharing information at the ground-troop level to make individual soldiers more autonomous. Since 1994, the DoD has used "after action reviews," debriefing sessions that record, digitize, and share troop experiences. It's an approach that recognizes that people on the front lines of battle hold the information that can establish the difference between success and failure, life and death. In a struggle for survival, the only truth that matters is "ground truth." Today's leading-edge organizations value and measure the "ground truth" that will help them succeed in a volatile and chaotic economy.

CHAPTER SIX

CUT COSTS, NOT VALUE

Rule #1: Never lose money.
Rule #2: Never forget Rule #1.

—Warren Buffet

When the dot-com bubble burst, thousands of technology companies went into panic mode, slashing staff, cutting perks, and dropping new products like so many proverbial hot potatoes. Jeff Allen, formerly COO and now CEO, of Intellispace, Inc. took a more thoughtful approach to cost cutting that protected his company's ability to survive and compete. In fact, Upside magazine named Intellispace, the world's first provider of managed optical Ethernet IP addresses, one of its 100 best private companies for 2001. Conferred by an advisory group of financial analysts and market researchers, the Upside award recognizes private companies for achievement, customer service, financial performance, and management experience.

Nevertheless, at the time that technology stocks started to slump, Intellispace was burning through $3 million a month.

Allen knew that worrying about reported profits or losses wasn't his first priority—he had to focus on the actual movement of cash. One of Allen's first moves was to institute just-in-time purchasing, eliminating the need for an expensive inventory of Internet routers. Other cost-savings measures quickly followed: renegotiation of supply contracts, trimming expansion plans, and austerity measures undertaken with full communication and collaboration with staff.

In the midst of this aggressive cost cutting, however, Allen protected and even expanded the organization's sales function, instituting a company-wide sales imperative: "Everyone sells. . . . The best way to help the company is to get people to buy our products," Allen recalls. "We weren't in a position where we could save our way into prosperity. We needed to keep growing revenue if we were going to build value."

Cutting costs while building and preserving value—that's the greatest financial challenge of leading in a chaotic economy.

In a turbulent economic environment, any company can experience slowed revenue growth, lowered earnings, and overall weakened financial health. Under these circumstances, not cutting costs is usually *not* an option. However, *how* you cut costs is every bit as important as *whether* you cut costs. Poorly designed and executed cost reductions can cut your organization's value as well as its expenses. In fact, organizations that sacrifice long-term competitiveness for short-term cost savings often do more damage to their viability than if they had done nothing at all.

To help you avoid this trap, we've provided the benchmark leaders' six rules for cost-cutting in volatile times. If your organization is facing a financial challenge, you should review these rules before you take any action. We developed them based on interviews and consulting projects involving hundreds of executives who have undertaken significant cost reductions. Some followed these rules throughout their cost-reduction efforts; others had to learn them the hard way. Once you learn them, you'll be able to identify how much you need to cut, how quickly you need to cut, and how you can cut while creating and building corporate value.

Rule 1: Confront Financial Reality

All leaders would love to see earnings that increase year after year. However, this goal is rarely realistic, even in the best of times. All businesses, like all economies, go through cycles that cause stagnation or decreases in revenue. At the same time, expenses, particularly labor costs, tend to remain stable or increase over time. Without an ever-vigilant eye, revenues can drift down while expenses creep up, and eventually the two collide.

Clearly, the role of leadership in a volatile economy is to head off that collision before it occurs. To do that, however, leaders must be willing and able to confront financial reality. After all, most leaders know the basics of financial management. Yet surprisingly few leaders follow them, whether out of denial, panic, arrogance, or some other reason. The leaders who persevere in challenging economic times are the ones who proactively confront and accept their financial situation.

If you think your organization might be facing a financial challenge, ask yourself the following questions: Do you know details of your current financial situation? Do you know whether your revenues are decreasing? Do you know whether your expenses are rising? Do you know when, and if, your expenses will exceed your revenues?

To help our clients answer these questions, we often perform an exercise by drawing a "financial reality" chart. This very simple chart helps visually represent financial reality in terms that everyone in the organization can understand. We recommend that you construct one, too.

To draw this chart, first plot past, present, and estimated future revenues. For the purposes of this exercise, going back two years and projecting forward two years will suffice. (No matter how grave the situation may be, it's important not to "pad" the figures to make the news more palatable. A little padding now will only distort decision-making later.) Second, plot your past, present, and future expenses along the same timeline. (We told you this was simple.)

Financial Reality

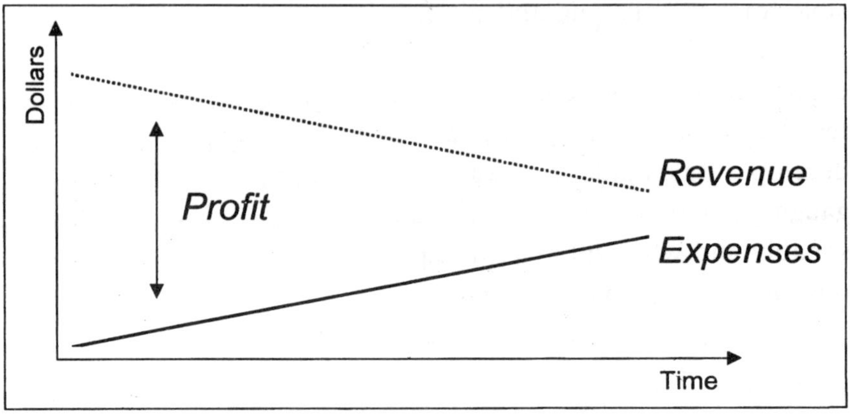

Once you have drawn these lines, two things become clear. First, a quick look should tell you the size of your challenge. The gap between your revenue and expense lines represents your profit from operations (if the revenue line is above the cost line; otherwise, this gap represents your losses). Second, the "profit gap" tells you how quickly you have to act. For example, if your profit gap has been shrinking for several months and will disappear completely in three months, you know you need to start moving.

Although this chart seems very simple, it's astounding how few organizations can produce it quickly. While some companies like Cisco can produce this chart on a daily basis (they actually have a one-day close of their monthly financials), most companies cannot. However, in a fluctuating economy, leaders need to have real-time access to the numbers if they're going to succeed. If you have trouble accessing these numbers, this may indicate that your financial systems need upgrading or decision rights are not appropriately allocated. In either event, your organization faces a much greater likelihood of reacting either too slowly or incorrectly.

Confronting financial reality isn't just for the leaders who will head cost-cutting interventions, however. All stakeholders must understand and accept what's happening to the organization. After all, people throughout the organization will be responsible for implementing and supporting any cost-cutting measures that may be necessary. If you use the financial reality chart to explain the situation concretely and objectively, you'll have a better chance of obtaining buy-in. The chart will also help you to develop a stakeholder relations plan for the turnaround effort. By gauging reaction to the chart, you can diagnose who will act reasonably and who will react in a panicked, paralyzed, contemptuous, or clueless mode. (See Rule #3.)

Rule 2: Confront Your Cash

Rule #2 is essentially a corollary to Rule #1; only this time, instead of charting revenues versus expenses, you're monitoring cash outflows versus cash inflows. It is entirely possible to be profitable and still have poor cash flow. (By cash flow, we mean real money flowing into, or out of, a company's bank account.) Boston Market, Montgomery Ward, and United Press International all operated profitably for many years, but ultimately filed for bankruptcy because they couldn't generate sufficient cash flow to cover their costs. How does this happen? Many situations can cause a cash crunch, but the following are some of the most common.

Growth

Ironically, growth can often cause a cash shortage. When earnings grow from expanding operations (rather than a reduction in costs or an increase in prices), companies often find themselves with a decreased cash flow. A growing company may increase its receivables, but it may also increase its expenses through wages, inventories, or other costs. Often these expenses are paid from cash at a much faster rate than receivables are converted into cash. In the absence of sufficient cash reserves, decreased cash flow can become negative cash flow—and without some outside funding, negative cash flow usually leads to bankruptcy.

Declining Stock Valuation

If your company's stock is publicly traded and its market value has dropped, you may find yourself strapped for cash. Let's say, for example, that your current business plan calls for growth through acquisitions. Let's also say that you've successfully undertaken acquisitions in the past and that you've historically used stock as your currency of choice to purchase other firms. As your stock is devalued, you may find potential acquirees less willing to take stock, or you may find yourself having to offer more stock than you'd like. In either event, you may have to switch to cash. If these cash expenditures are unexpected, you may find that you're spending more cash than you had set aside, potentially leading to cash shortfalls.

Failure to Replace Investment Cash with Revenues

Another dangerous situation occurs when organizations fail—through poor planning or poor performance—to replace investment cash with cash from revenues. Perhaps no business situation better exemplifies this problem than the recent dot-com bust. Companies like Pets.com, Buy.com, and DrKoop.com all had huge burn rates with little apparent plan for offsetting the burn with cash inflows. At one point, DrKoop.com was burning through the cash raised in its IPO so fast that from June 30 to September 30, 1999, outflows for expenses totaled $24 million while revenues were a paltry $2.9 million.

One particularly interesting situation occurs when a company has more cash than market capitalization. Drugstore.com, for example, had $130 million in cash (as of Spring 2001) with a market capitalization of only $80 million. What's driving this strange discrepancy? According to Aram J. Fuchs, CEO at Fertilemind.net, a New York equity research firm: "Investors believe that Drugstore's management will blow through the remaining cash and end up closing operations."

Unwise Debt Incursion

Another problem occurs when organizations drain cash or incur debt to "cover up" unprofitable operations. Hospitals are a particularly notorious example of this problem. Some hospitals lose money from operations, but hide this problem from their stakeholders by drawing on large cash reserves or by leveraging their large asset base to take on unhealthy amounts of debt. As the commercials for Discover Card warn: "Just because you have the power, doesn't mean you should use it. Spend your credit wisely."

Investment in Low-Return Projects

Hospitals often exemplify another cash problem: spending cash to invest in low-return projects. Sometimes organizations will "loosen" their required return-on-investment criteria and spend precious cash for projects whose returns are specious at best. Misaligned incentives, unchecked egos, or self interest can all cause an executive team to look at doomed-from-the-start projects through rose-colored glasses. Unfortunately, when organizations like hospitals, retailers, or manufacturers use cash to build a new state-of-the-art facility to go after unprofitable markets, illiquidity is likely to follow.

The lesson from these situations? Profit is good, but cash converted from profit is even better. Confront your cash reality now by remembering the following:

1. Anticipate your upcoming cash expenditures, i.e., anticipate capital expenditures, increases in expenses, acquisitions, etc.
2. In times of uncertainty, conserve cash whenever possible. In particular, watch special expenses. Cash crunches often come with short-term cash outflows to finance projects with "distant future" cash inflows. Make especially sure that such projects have a positive and timely expected return on investment.
3. Sometimes you may need to go outside the firm for cash to survive. While financing costs can be high, the costs imposed

on your organization by teetering on the edge of illiquidity can be even higher.

4. If you choose debt to raise cash, you face not only the obvious financial expenses (e.g., interest payments), but also the continuing drain on cash that could prevent future investment.
5. Achieve balance between the payment of payables and the conversion of receivables to cash. If cash expenditures far exceed the conversion of receivables to cash (and it often does), this can lead to a serious cash crunch. In times of cash shortfalls, you can use vendors as de facto lenders by delaying payment, but this can be expensive (particularly in terms of late fees and lost discounts) and can damage relationships with key business partners (which entails its own set of costs).
6. Financial markets, whether the stock market or your local bank or bond-rating agencies, like solid cash positions. In times of volatility, companies with strong cash positions will command better analyst ratings, bond ratings, investor support, and borrowing rates.

Rule 3:
Assess and Manage Leadership Reaction

The first two rules seem simple and straightforward, but every day the news is filled with stories of organizations that didn't follow them. The unfortunate reality is that many leaders react to crisis by tossing the rulebook out the window. While the fundamentals of managing money may be entirely rational, leaders in a volatile economy are often anything but.

Benchmark leaders remember that any financial challenge quickly becomes an intensely personal crisis for everyone in the organization. Managers worry that somehow they have failed—or will fail—and thus lose their jobs. Employees worry that their heads will roll under the cost-cutter's ax. All of these fears can drive irrational decisions that only make the situation worse.

Therefore, before leaders react to the operational opportunities of a financial challenge, they must first address the emotional ones.

We use the Leadership Action/Reality Grid to assess and manage leadership reactions to a financial challenge. The chart demonstrates that *how* leaders react to financial reality is just as important as whether they acknowledge its existence. Some leaders panic at the prospect of slowing revenues and immediately start slashing and burning their operations. Other leaders refuse to take any action, preferring to pretend this unwanted data doesn't exist. Still other leaders accept the "financial reality" chart, evaluate their costs carefully, look for expenditures unrelated to their mission, and then start cutting.

Almost without fail, it is this last group of leaders—the thoughtful yet decisive leaders—who achieve the greatest success. These leaders confront reality and then take action in a way that preserves their company's ability to compete. While they can cut deeply, these leaders know to cut resources that aren't directly contributing to the fulfillment of their mission. Therefore, they're able to preserve their company's competitive advantage.

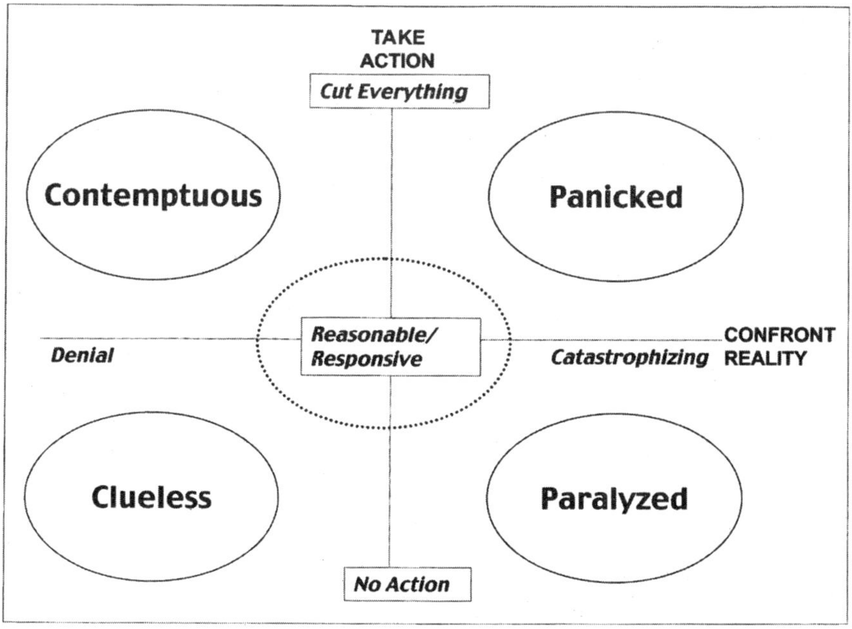

What sets these leaders apart is their "reasonableness" and willingness to act. They don't ignore reality, nor do they subscribe to worst-case-scenario pessimism. They don't avoid making necessary cuts, nor do they swing the ax without thinking. The key to being in this "Reasonable/Responsive" category is to understand your natural reactions to stressful situations, manage those reactions, and then act appropriately.

When Panicked and Paralyzed leaders receive bad news, they quickly extrapolate the worst possible scenarios: A revenue slowdown of 10 percent quickly becomes the death of a product line, or an increase in expenses spells the end of competitiveness. In any organization, someone always assumes this "Chicken Little" role, and his or her catastrophizing and fear-mongering have led many executive teams to make some very bad decisions. (One reason for drawing the "financial reality" chart is to keep focused on the facts and avoid unfounded speculation.) Although both Panicked and Paralyzed leaders fall onto the "catastrophizing" end of the grid, they differ in their ability to act. The Panicked leader reacts to catastrophizing thoughts with excessive slashing, while the Paralyzed leader freezes and becomes unable to do anything.

On the other end of the "confront reality" spectrum are Clueless and Contemptuous leaders. Although neither group is likely to be reading this book, you may encounter both somewhere in your organization. The Contemptuous leaders are those who ignore the reality facing the organization, but for one reason or another, find themselves in a perpetual slash-and-burn mode. It's not uncommon for leaders in this category to have nicknames like "killer" or "axman" or something equally gruesome. Then there are those who are neither aware of the reality facing their companies nor in any mood to take action (a.k.a. Clueless). Their motto is "ignorance is bliss"—until they lose their jobs.

Of the four types of ineffective leaders, Clueless and Paralyzed leaders are useless in difficult times because they do nothing to manage costs. Panicked and Contemptuous leaders, on the other hand, present a more immediate danger because they go too far and cut value along with costs.

The scenario for Panicked and Contemptuous leaders goes like this: Panicked executives don't confront reality until it confronts them. Well into a downturn, they finally realize that expenses have exceeded revenues. Then, in a state of panic, these executives start slashing wildly, closing departments or plants, laying off workers, and ceasing investments in vital operations. (For Contemptuous leaders, this approach is standard operating procedure.)

By cutting every cost they can think of, these leaders ultimately destroy the company's core resources and its ability to compete. Ironically, because the cuts were so ill conceived, they leave "100% of the work for 80% of the people." This situation undermines the organization's performance and staff morale, creating a "backlash" pressure to refill the positions at any cost. Like a crash diet gone wrong, the organization rapidly adds on "expense weight," which, in turn, precipitates additional cycles of cost-cutting.

Binge/Purge Approach to Cost-Cutting

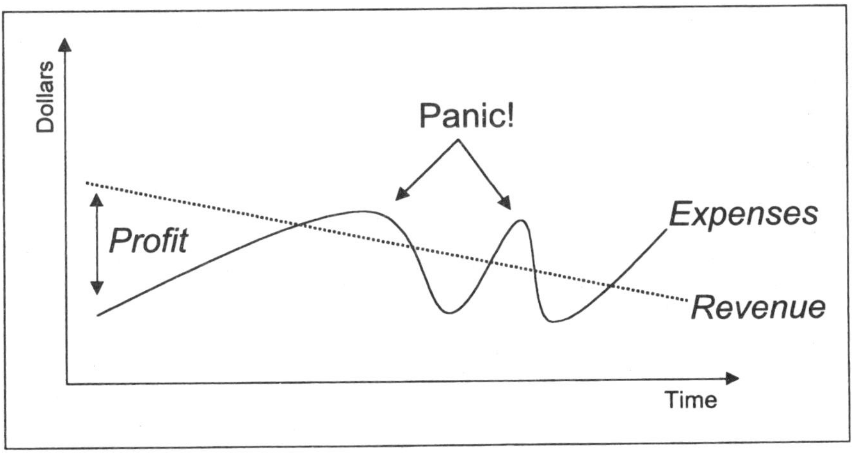

This binge/purge approach to cost-cutting leaves the organization in a weakened state, underinvesting in the things that make it successful, i.e., people, technology, R&D, and marketing. Underinvestment ultimately leads to a poor competitive position, as a wealth of research demonstrates. One lesson from our personal experience is especially telling: In a 1993 study of 281 hospitals, we found that hospitals that undertook the binge/purge approach to cost-cutting experienced an increased in patient mortality rates. Not only did these organizations endanger their own viability, they also jeopardized the lives of their customers.

Rule 4: Pick High-Return Opportunities

Cutting too deeply is one way leaders can undermine their organization's value. The opposite approach—making insignificant cost reductions—can be just as detrimental.

We are all familiar with the "Dilbert-esque" austerity measures that many organizations undertake: Minimize paperclip usage, switch to a cheaper brand of coffee, or mandate that the cafeteria staff slice the cheese and bacon more thinly. Employees find these actions so amusing and, at times, infuriating because they usually consume more resources than they save. Such cost-cutting efforts become "low-return" when they incur enough project-related costs to negate any potential savings. These concealed costs come in two main forms: the cost of management and team-member time to plan and implement the project, and the cost associated with low morale and lost employee goodwill.

That's not to say that you can't save money in the cafeteria; however, any savings must outweigh the project-related costs. For example, constant memos and meetings to encourage cafeteria workers to use two ounces of meat instead of three are probably not worth the effort. Reconfiguring the cafeteria layout or redesigning the food-prep process just might be. You can't be sure which activities will be worthwhile until you conduct a cost-benefit analysis of your options.

When selecting cost-reduction opportunities, the key is to not get diverted by minutiae, but to focus on those issues that are likely to generate the greatest returns. Particularly in times of economic uncertainty, leadership time is at a premium and must be reserved for decisions that truly impact the bottom line.

Rule 5: Spend to Save

Sometimes you need to spend money to save money. Investments in information technology, process redesign, certain types of training, and other programs can deliver returns far in excess of the initial investment. Unfortunately, it's easy to overlook these investments in the midst of a cost-cutting frenzy.

Even in volatile times, benchmark leaders invest in programs and systems that drive down costs and drive up productivity. Disney, for example, invested more than $20 million in an online system that will allow employees to make their supply purchases via the Web. While some executives may have balked at the initial cost, Disney projects the system will save $40 million annually. Apache Corporation, a company that produces natural gas and crude oil, invested in a $20-million alarm system for its oil wells that warns technicians of problems significant enough to cause a shutdown. Now Apache can proactively avert shutdowns and thus increase oil production.

Of course, sometimes a challenge is so severe that any immediate expenditure may become an impossible burden. In that case, the challenge is to get revenues and expenses under control for the short term, and then begin to reevaluate opportunities for cost-reduction systems that will generate a high long-term return on investment.

Rule 6: Don't Wait to Cut

High-performing leaders know you don't have to wait for a downturn to address your costs. Cutting costs during the good times can offer two significant advantages in the tough times. First, there tends to be less price sensitivity during good times than during bad times, which means there's often less cost-based competition. This means that every dollar you save by reducing costs goes to your bottom line, and ultimately to your coffers. And as we noted before, tough times favor those with deep pockets. Second, tough times can often entail price wars, and whoever has the lowest costs will win a price war.

In 2001, the PC industry hit its worst slump ever. Not counting Dell, the industry reported over $1 billion in losses. Dell, on the other hand, reported profits close to $400 million. How? During all of the previous boom years, while PC makers like Compaq and Gateway were enjoying the good times, Dell was acting as if the boom could end at any moment. They ratcheted down their costs, with key investments in technology, process improvements, and a cost-driven culture. Not only did they greatly strengthen their cash position, but when the boom times ended, their cost curve was a lot lower than their competitors'. This meant they could declare an all-out price war (which they did), and their competitors simply would not be able to keep up (they couldn't). So far it's worked—Dell is now the world's number-one PC maker.

Case Studies: Bringing the Rules to Life

For this section, we've chosen to illustrate and integrate the lessons of the benchmark leaders with case studies from two large, well-known organizations. Both organizations showed enough depth and breadth in their cost-cutting to highlight the six rules and offer practical strategies for cost reduction that other leaders can adopt in their own organizations.

Cisco: Leveraging Technology for Productivity

Larry Carter, Chief Financial Officer of Cisco, is not your average bean counter. While he is one of the few "graybeards" at Cisco, currently in his mid-fifties, he is also one of the most visionary and technologically savvy CFOs around.

Carter has a remarkable talent for making investments in systems and technologies that offer great returns in the form of significant cost reductions. Even in the midst of economic volatility and uncertainty, Cisco has maintained its commitment to making sizable upfront investments in systems that it knows will drive long-term profitability. These include investments in systems for financial efficiency, technical support, outsourcing, purchasing, accounts payable, and payroll.

When Carter joined Cisco in 1996, the company was awash with acquisitions. While the operational integrations were going well, Cisco was barely keeping up with the management of its own financials. Carter knew that the systems needed to be made more effective, but he also knew that a quick technology fix wasn't the answer. He stated upfront that "maintaining the status quo just wasn't acceptable," and then hired finance managers who had experience with process improvements. In purchasing and accounts payable, for example, Carter consolidated the two departments under one manager with the vision of redesigning the entire "procurement process." By undertaking a thorough review of process flow, they eliminated a large number of paper-based transactions, opting instead for a model of "networked commerce." Then Carter made sure that once they had redesigned the areas, they actually made the necessary staff changes to realize their savings. Since this change, they've reduced their accounts payable and purchasing headcount, with productivity improvements in each area of 55 percent and 33 percent, respectively.

In the area of technical support, Cisco has been an industry leader since its founding. But with well over a million incoming phone calls a year, Cisco knew there had to be potential opportunities to improve productivity in tech support. The challenge became "how to offer the same high level of support while simultaneously maximizing productivity." The solution was to treat its customers as partners. Using a Web-centric model, customer support can now be handled via the Web, rather than by phone. Not only does this offer the customer greater flexibility in obtaining technical support, but Cisco's Controller, Dennis Powell, estimates that this system has also reduced incoming telephone calls by more than 75,000 per month. Customers can also download the software they need, helping Cisco avoid the costs associated with physical shipments. Currently, about 90 percent of software requests are handled and fulfilled via Web-enabled downloads. This has been about more than just short-term cost cutting, however. Powell recently noted, "For us, it's about figuring out how productive we can be with the people we have. We are very passionate about leveraging technology to improve productivity."

At the time of this writing, it's easy to criticize technology companies for continuing to invest in equipment and information systems. Nevertheless, Carter's approach is sound because it maintains Cisco's long-term competitive advantage. Cisco's advanced financial management systems demonstrate its commitment to confronting financial reality; sticking to its core objectives in the face of adversity demonstrates a reasonable leadership mindset; and its "spend to save" approach to productivity improvement shows a concern for preserving the long-term value, despite swings in stock value.

With their CFO leading from the front, Cisco's executives insist that productivity needs to improve by 5 percent every year. Carter's team has developed an effective system of merging process improvements, Internet and information technology, and the discipline to cut poor-performing projects. This combination of eliminating inefficiencies—while improving its ability to service its customers—has been an important driver of Cisco's striking financial performance. It also explains why Cisco is likely to weather current market volatility much better than its competitors.

Campbell's: Cutting Costs from Soup to Nuts

At Campbell's Soup Company, "thinking outside the can" has generated cost-management initiatives that are a core part of the company's growth strategy. The $6-billion food giant has been in the top quartile in earnings growth in the food industry for six years—and wants to stay there, courtesy of its cost-optimization program. "It isn't about headcount elimination or cutting for the sake of taking costs to the bottom line," says Dale Morrison,

CEO. "We call cost-cutting a productivity program enabler, because it is proving the investment resources we need to grow the business."

CFO Basil Anderson has led the cost-optimization program to savings of more than $450 million, most of it by reducing costs across divisions and product lines. One sweet idea involved setting up a global chocolate task force involving all divisions that use chocolate, including such brands as Godiva and Pepperidge Farms. Using centralized chocolate purchasing, Campbell's has realized more than $4 million in cost savings.

In addition to negotiating lower costs, Campbell's is redesigning processes to drive costs even lower. "If you simply go out and negotiate a lower price for flour, that's short-term," Anderson explains. "We save a lot more money by changing where and how we make things." In 1996, the company streamlined its soup production by cutting the number of soup lines. It also standardized and centralized its juice and sauce manufacturing into two plants, reducing the number of suppliers from around 40 to 2.

Another cost-savings mechanism requires managers to focus on what the company does most cost-effectively. When Campbell's was the lone runner for dominance in the soup market, it made sense to raise its own chickens and make its own cans. That's no longer true in today's world of ever-more-nimble competitors. So Allen engineered the sale of Campbell's poultry business. By purchasing poultry from the supplier, Campbell's saved $4 million—in addition to the cash they raised from the sale. Perhaps Anderson's most radical move was the sale of the can-making division, which had been an integral part of Campbell's operations for years, but was no longer cost-effective. The $123-million deal enabled Campbell's to realize its goal of using the least possible amount of capital to produce sales.

"What we do with the savings is what matters," says Anderson. "Cost reduction by itself doesn't create the most value. The issue is what you do with the proceeds and how you reinvest them back into our brands—that's what really drives shareholder wealth."

Perhaps no one better demonstrates a reasonable willingness to confront financial reality than an organization like Campbell's, which continually evaluates the profitability of its products and divisions. While other organizations irrationally hold onto obsolete product lines, Campbell's makes the difficult decision to focus on its strengths and let its suppliers and competitors focus on theirs. In the process of selling less competitive divisions, they also generate a cash cushion that helps them weather market volatility. And by positioning cost-reduction as a productivity enhancer, Campbell's creates the sort of corporate value that ensures long-term success.

Practical Strategies for Cutting Costs, Not Value

From the case studies, we can see that leading-edge companies like Cisco and Campbell's use cost-reduction techniques as a way to maintain their competitive advantage. Here's how you can emulate their practices:

- **Leverage technology.** While it requires an initial upfront investment, technology remains one of the most effective ways to drive costs out of an organization. However, as much as the right technology can streamline functions and improve productivity, a poorly chosen technological solution can create waste and frustration in the organization. When considering technology, remember to focus on areas of significance and submit every acquisition to the return-on-investment test.
- **Cut costs across silos.** Cost reduction is everyone's responsibility, not just that of a failing division or department. As Campbell's and Cisco demonstrate, redesigning processes across the organization generates economies of scale that often outdo what any one leader could do alone.
- **Invest in interchangeable parts.** Cisco, Campbell's, and other high-performing organizations continually reinvent and

reconfigure themselves to reduce costs and build value. As a younger, more growth-oriented company, Cisco acquires new capabilities by acquiring other organizations. With a longer history and more "baggage," Campbell's has streamlined operations by selling production capabilities to suppliers. Of course, neither action should be undertaken lightly, since any sale or acquisition raises the possibility of job losses or culture clashes. Nevertheless, in turbulent times, benchmark leaders focus on the good of the whole over the security of the parts.

A Parting Message: Beware of Underinvestment

One common thread runs through the rules, case studies, and strategies: The aim of cost-cutting is not the dollars per se, but the reallocation of resources for future growth and competitiveness. The true test of effective leadership is not how deeply you cut in response to an immediate financial challenge, but how well you prepare your organization to face the next challenge . . . and the next . . . and the next. In volatile times, remember to protect, preserves, and shore up those things that are crucial to your customers to preserve, your competitive advantage.

If you need to reduce expenses, remember the most important cost—the cost of underinvestment. As we said earlier, underinvestment means cutting back on the things that make you successful, and its ultimate cost to your organization is immeasurably high. Remember McDonnell Douglas, which spent much of the mid-1990s slashing and burning to kick-start profitability. While they saw some short-term profit payoffs from this approach, many analysts think it also eroded McDonnell's long-term ability to compete. As one writer for *Fortune* put it: "Years of underinvestment turned McDonnell into the RC Cola of airplanes—third place in a two-way race."

CHAPTER SEVEN

OUTPOSITION YOUR COMPETITORS

I'm often credited with the motto, "Only the paranoid survive." I have no idea when I first said this, but the fact remains that, when it comes to business, I believe in the value of paranoia. Business success contains the seeds of its own destruction. The more successful you are, the more people want a chunk of your business and then another chunk and then another until there is nothing left. I believe that the prime responsibility of a manager is to guard constantly against other people's attacks and to inculcate this guardian attitude in the people under his or her management.

—Andy Grove
Only the Paranoid Survive

Custom Surfaces, Inc., a leading fabricator of custom solid surfaces and countertops for residential and commercial buildings, could see it coming. New home construction was slowing, sales at home stores were down, and new offices weren't being built so quickly. After years of riding volatility's upside, with tremendous rates of growth and an industry-leading position, it was now about to be confronted with its downside. But Rick Smith, CEO, wasn't about to start shrinking the company: "I told our team we face two realities. First, the overall market is slowing and we need to accept that. But second, we will not stop growing, regardless of what the market does." The message was clear: Custom Surfaces needed to outposition its competitors to take a greater share of a shrinking market.

Its first step was understanding what its competitors were up to. If Custom Surfaces was losing business to anyone, it wanted to know why. While Custom Surfaces wasn't losing much business—it was the leader in its markets—for its highly competitive senior team, any loss was too much. What it found was somewhat surprising. While its Custom Surfaces' finished products (i.e., installed solid surfaces) were better than its competitors—it had the lowest number of warranty claims—customers thought its competitors offered a more comprehensive array of sales services.

Ironically, Custom Surfaces had worked and invested to ensure that its pre-sales services were far more efficient and streamlined than its competitors'. Jim Young, COO, said, "We have unmatched pre-sales technological capabilities, with state-of-the-art measuring and installation systems. But we discovered that in many cases, our technology was moving us too quickly. We were so focused on being efficient and technically expert, that we missed that some customers were more interested in a dialogue with us."

Armed with insight about its competitive strengths and weaknesses, Smith and Young moved quickly to reposition their offering. They didn't waste time trying to redo areas where their customers already saw them as dominant, but instead worked to enhance their offerings in the areas that seemed weaker. This meant improving Custom Surfaces' pre-sales services by spending more time with clients. When the company coupled increased time with the customer with its stronger product, not only did it reverse customer perceptions about its weaknesses, but customers gained an even greater respect and appreciation for the company's strengths. For Custom Surfaces, more time with the customers meant more time to showcase its other competitive advantages.

The strategy worked. Sales continue to grow—Custom Surfaces recently posted its best month ever—and losses to competitors have decreased. Young noted, "When the market tightens, understanding where you stand relative to your competitors, and then turning that understanding into competitive victories, is critical. Just being innovative and creative isn't enough. If you can't translate that innovativeness into a closed sale and a satisfied customer, you won't survive."

To survive during turbulent times, leaders must be serious about outpositioning their competitors. Competitors can come in many forms: another company, scientific or technological change, a market shift, time, or customer perceptions. But, regardless of the type of competition, it represents a threat to the stability of your organization. The reality of volatile times, as Andy Grove noted, is that someone or something is after you. And, if you don't figure out who or what it is, how it might take your business, and just how big of a threat it represents, there may not be a company left to reposition by the time you do figure it out.

Those who don't prepare for turbulent times—those who aren't just a little bit paranoid—may not survive. How can you outposition your competitors so you can compete more effectively in a "survival of the fittest" business environment? The leaders in our study offer the following advice.

Rule 1: Measure Demand

What if you threw a party and nobody came? That's a risk leaders face during volatile times: Organizations can't compete for a pool of dollars that isn't there. If no demand exists for an offering—or the demand exists, but is met thoroughly by others—then your organization should focus its energies elsewhere.

Of course, world-class visionary organizations seem to invent the future by developing products for which a demand does not yet exist. But there is a big difference between latent demand and no demand. In the first case, the demand is there, but unacknowledged; waiting for just the right offering. In the second case, the demand is acknowledged, but it's been turned down. There was latent demand for the PC—people had always wanted faster information, but until the right product (i.e., the PC) came along, the demand lay dormant. Broccoli-flavored bubble gum, on the other hand, has no demand. And hopefully, it never will.

Measuring demand is a seemingly simple, but absolutely critical step for one reason: In volatile times, demand for an offering can disappear. And if the demand for your offering vanishes, you will need to exit that business. Once you realize the demand just isn't there anymore, the sooner you exit the business, the more money you will have to invest somewhere else (e.g., another business or division or product). It can be a bitter pill to swallow that there just isn't a demand for your offering, but facing the situation honestly can help you live to fight another day.

Rule 2: Know the Competition

In addition to knowing your customer base, you must also know your competitors. Whether you look at business, politics, sports, or any other endeavor, history is filled with examples of leaders who failed because *they did not recognize a competitor until it was too late*. In volatile times, the competition is tough enough when you see them coming. Imagine how hard it gets when you're hit with no apparent warning.

In order to compete effectively, you must understand who you're competing against. It sounds simple, but defining your competition is actually more complicated than it seems, especially since competition comes in many hidden forms. To help you identify your competitors, especially the not-so-obvious ones, we've defined the four main types.

One classic type of competitor is the *Obvious Rival.* These competitors are so named because their rivalry is direct, longstanding, and readily apparent. Some classic competitors include the following: McDonald's vs. Burger King; Coke vs. Pepsi; Xerox vs. Canon; Kodak vs. Fuji; Intel vs. AMD; BMW vs. Mercedes; Dell vs. Compaq; Ben and Jerry's vs. Häagen Dazs. If your organization is well established, you probably have a clear idea of who your obvious rivals are.

Another category of rival is the *Upstart Rival.* These are firms that escape their competitors' scrutiny due to their small size or novelty. Whether you have upstart rivals, or you are an upstart rival, the size of the competitive radar screen (i.e., the scope of competitive intelligence gathering) will determine your success or failure. If you're the upstart rival, staying off your competitors' radar screen can be critical to gaining enough of a toehold in the market to become a serious threat. If you're competing against the upstart rival, it's important to identify them as a threat as quickly as possible. For example, Kodak left Fuji off its radar screen for far too long. Fuji grabbed 1 percent, then 2 percent, then 4 percent, and then 8 percent of the American film market before Kodak began to consider Fuji as a competitor. But by then, Fuji had a significant presence in the market and was well on its way to becoming a full-blown obvious rival. For Kodak, the radar screen was too small. For Fuji, it was just right.

The third, less obvious form of competitor forces you to look beyond your Obvious Rivals and Upstart Rivals to industries or firms that haven't even been created yet. These competitors are *Unforeseen Rivals* because they emerge from major market shifts that are outside of an organization's normal monitoring system. For example, it's doubtful that Merrill Lynch initially saw Charles Schwab as a competitive threat or that most banks took E* Trade seriously when it started out. As technological and scientific innovation continues to drive our volatile economy, unforeseen rivals will play an increasingly large part in the changing competitive landscape.

The *Nothing* is perhaps the most formidable of all of your competitors. Many leaders miss this as a rival, thinking that if they haven't lost a sale to a competing organization, they haven't really lost. Unfortunately, nothing could be further from the truth. As the rock band Rush said, "If you choose not to decide, you still have made a choice." If your potential customers choose not to purchase anything, it's because doing nothing offers them greater value than your products or services. That should be the most powerful and motivating message of all.

Rule 3: Evaluate Your Competitive Positioning

Assessing your customers and competitors helps you better understand what you're competing for, and who you're competing against. The next challenge is to differentiate yourself from your competitors so you can capture your customers' attention and thus their business.

Unfortunately, many leaders attempt to differentiate themselves based on a limited range of options—usually some combination of just price or quality. While this seems like an easy way to assess your position relative to your competitors, there are two major problems with it. First, you may take actions that you didn't need to take. For example, if you think you're competing just on price, but customers are, in fact, relatively insensitive to price, any price cuts you initiate may just give away profit. Second, you may overlook or ignore an unbeatable competitive advantage. A manufacturer of drilling equipment for oil rigs experienced this. While it was attacking its competitors with the technical superiority of its equipment (e.g., more g-forces, greater conductance, etc.), an analysis discovered that customers were much more driven by the life of the product. This was a shock, especially because the company had almost dropped the product life issue from its competitive assessment for its presumed unimportance. And, while this firm had a slight advantage on the technical issues, it had a huge competitive advantage in product life. Recognizing this previously-ignored advantage helped generate a 35-percent revenue increase in just one year.

As this last example shows, the reality of competitive positioning is much richer than just price or quality. In fact, our studies have identified *seven* key dimensions of competition. By analyzing their performance on these seven dimensions, leaders are better able to differentiate themselves from their competitors. And, particularly in a turbulent economy, competitive differentiation is the key to competitive success. It's a case where a little more rigorous analysis upfront provides a dramatically better solution down the line. To help leaders with this process, we've developed a technique we call Competitive Dimensions Analysis (CDA). The following overview of CDA provides a list of issues that you should consider when positioning your organization during chaotic times. As you review each of the seven dimensions, think about how your organization stacks up against your competition.

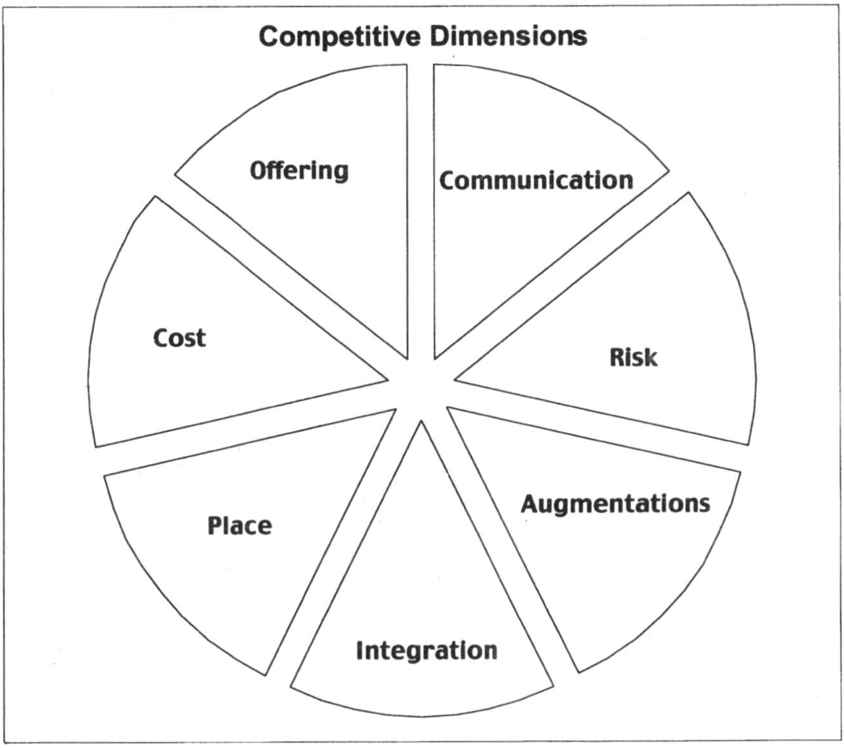

Cost

Cost is, of course, one of the most fundamental dimensions of competition. It is more than just price, however. Cost is any outlay of time, money, effort, etc., on the part of the customer in order to acquire your offering.

As you think about the price of your offerings, you might also want to consider customers' cost of financing. Payment periods, credit terms, etc., are all part of the total financial outlay for customers. If two systems both have prices of $100,000, but one has 90-day payment terms while the other has 30, the first system offers a de facto discount of several thousand dollars because of potential investment returns over the extra 60 days.

You should also consider the costs of finding your product, switching to it from a competing product, and integrating it into your customers' existing business (for B2B companies) or lives (for direct-to-consumer.) Why has it been difficult for non-Windows PC operating systems to gain any serious foothold? For one reason, it is costly for customers to convert all of their systems (and perhaps their vendors' and key customers' systems, too) to a new platform. Someone could offer a new operating system for a few hundred dollars, but it would require their customers to spend thousands, if not millions, on hardware, programming, and retraining.

Offering

Your offering, whether it's a product or service, has qualities that distinguish it from your competitors. These qualities range from the subtle (such as colors or packaging) to the significant (such as technical superiority). In fact, the latter is probably the most important differentiator of an offering. *Technical superiority* answers the question: Whose product/service is better at providing the desired benefit? With televisions, for example, you can measure technical superiority in color and clarity. If you're evaluating website design services, you can look at proposed designs for speed of loading, artistry, debugging, programming language, etc. *Quality* goes hand-in-hand with technical superiority. Customers want to know if there are any defects in your offering. If you promise technical superiority, will the offering deliver?

Of course, no one will continue to buy a product or service—even a high-quality, superior one—that is frustrating to use. For this reason, *ease of use* has a huge impact on customers' willingness to purchase, often to the point of overriding other factors. Many people are willing to pay a premium for convenience, for everything from dry cleaning to food to laptops.

In addition to these basic issues of superiority, quality, and ease of use, highly competitive offerings have other qualities that add to their appeal. What about *variety* and *flexibility*? How many different options do customers have when purchasing your offering? Can they reconfigure it based on their unique needs?

Does your product offer *features* that appeal to a broad range of customers? Who offers more bells and whistles—you or the competition? Does one ERP system offer more modules than another? Does one car have more gadgets for the driver than another?

Also consider *scalability*: Will the offering grow with customers? Will the car brand your customer drives offer the same prestige when she's CEO of the company as it did when she worked in the mailroom? Will your network accommodate 30,000 PCs as well as it did 30?

Lastly, consider *packaging*. Most people consider packing important only in consumer products, and not B2B products or services. However, even B2B offerings are "packaged" with such things as corporate mottoes and icons, office space design, wardrobes, etc. What does your packaging say about you?

Communication

Businesses that can reach their customers with clear, compelling, and distinctive sales messages are much more successful than those that can't. Are you reaching your customers? Do they understand what you're selling? Do they know why they should buy it? One of the key factors that drives communication success is penetration—getting to the people who need to hear your message. What is the clarity of that message: Is it easily understood? What about frequency? Are you communicating frequently enough to ensure that customers don't forget your message?

Risk

Offerings with a strong competitive advantage are those that minimize risk for the purchaser. Therefore, you should ask yourself these questions: What personal or organizational risk is associated with the purchase of a particular offering? Will your product or service work, and how severely will it hurt the customer if it doesn't?

When evaluating the risk of buying an offering, customers primarily consider its reputation and their trust in that reputation. *Reputation* is the extent to which a brand or organization is well known. Is your offering still in the early-adopter stage, or is it well established? *Trust in brand* is the extent to which consumers believe your brand offers value. Is yours a brand that means quality? Are you BMW or Yugo? If you say you offer quality, do you back it up with a warranty or service agreement?

Of course, reputation can change with the *health of your organization.* A colleague of ours has a rule that she will never fly on airlines in financial trouble, for obvious reasons. As an airline nears bankruptcy, it will likely face underinvestment problems (such as cutting costs via the maintenance crew). Not every business faces this customer bias, but yours might.

Even when a company has a solid reputation, there is always some *outcome uncertainty* associated with a purchase. There's no way to sample an airline flight, but you can demo a new stereo system and test-drive a car. Can you eliminate some of the outcome uncertainty associated with your offerings?

Product Augmentations

In addition to the quality of your product or service, what other extensions add value to the original offering? Some of the most common product augmentations include training, service, pre-sales need assessment, technical support, free delivery and installation, etc. All of these product augmentations offer added value to customers that might tip the scales in your favor.

Integration

Consider how easy it is to integrate your offering with everything else the customer is already doing. Specifically, does it *fit with current state*: Does your offering support what your customer is currently doing? For example, does your ERP system fit with their current IT infrastructure? Are you selling personalized banking services to people who do their transactions online? What about *fit with future state*: Does your offering fit with what your customer has planned? Where does your product fit in the *sequencing* of a purchase? Does the organization have to do something else first before customers can purchase your offering? Must customers have a particular operating system, for example, before they can buy your word-processing applications?

Flow point is another important consideration. Can you be shut out because your competitors control key decision points in the marketing and sales process? Even if your competitors have an inferior offering, can they bundle their similar offering with a larger bundle of offerings for which they already have contracts? An executive from one of the world's largest group-purchasing organizations recently told us, "As long as our overall basket of products beats our competitors, we can have a few products within that basket that are inferior on a case-by-case basis."

Place

Place defines where and how you present your offerings to customers. Businesses have many choices regarding place, and in the era of the Internet, each choice has especially profound implications for the entire business model.

One critical consideration is geography. Ask yourself: regional, national, or international? How many locations or offices? On the Net or not—or most likely, online to what extent? Other critical factors include your *distribution channels and models*: Do customers buy your offering online, via a sales force, or in retail outlets? Are your offerings available via intermediaries or direct to consumer? If you use intermediaries, do they provide extra customer service that justifies the additional cost?

The point of these questions about place is to determine the level of customer *access*. In other words, do you make your offerings available in ways that fit customers' preferences and limitations? Although Charles Schwab is primarily an on-line broker, for example, they found that geographies with physical offices had approximately five times more sales than geographies without a physical presence. Consequently, while they're still a dominant online presence, they currently have more than 350 offices around the country.

This list of issues has probably given you a general idea of your position vis-â-vis your competitors. However, the risks of leading in volatile and chaotic times require leaders to have comprehensive, in-depth knowledge of their competitive position. Therefore, we recommend that you use quantitative measures to analyze these seven dimensions whenever possible. If you're assessing Cost, for example, simply saying, "Our terms are better" is insufficient. The CDA is most effective when you "harden" those measures into concrete numbers. This data, in turn, will help you identify strategies to differentiate yourself from your competitors.

Rule 4: Let Your Mission Guide Your Strategy—and Vice Versa

After conducting a Competitive Dimensions Analysis, you should have a solid picture of your competitive strengths, weaknesses, and opportunities. You also have a de facto assessment of where your competitors could attack you most successfully. When it comes time to act on these opportunities and outposition your competitors, you have a variety of strategies from which to choose. The option or mix of options you select will depend on your organization's mission. For example, if quality and personalized service are the dominating themes of your mission, you may not wish to pursue an opportunity to compete on the basis of lower costs and lower quality. Or if you are content with running a neighborhood bodega, you may not pursue the same strategy as a regional supermarket chain. Based on your mission and the results of your CDA, consider the following strategies for outpositioning your competition.

Seize the Advantage of Inimitability

Let's say that you've just completed the CDA and found that your offering is competitively superior in the areas of price, technical superiority, and geography. Let's also say that you've measured demand and found that these three issues are important to your customers. You're probably feeling pretty good, right?

Well, that's probably an appropriate attitude in the short term. But the next question you should ask yourself is: How long do I have before my competitors can replicate these advantages? All organizations compete against time. Given enough time, your competitors can reduce their costs to lower their price, improve their offering's technical performance, and open locations right next door to yours, ending your competitive advantage. If your product is *inimitable*, on the other hand, your competitors will never be more than second best.

There are three sources of inimitability; the first is available to anyone, while the other two tend to favor established organizations. The first source of inimitability is uniqueness. If your advantage is one-of-a-kind, such as a patent or a particular location, it is much harder to replicate than something as simple as a low price. A second source of inimitability is what economists call path dependency. This means that competitive advantage is gained over time through a sequence of events/actions that are difficult to replicate with just one action. For example, Memorial Sloan-Kettering Cancer Center's reputation is not something that competitors can easily usurp; it was built over many years of providing technically and psycho-socially superior service. A third source of inimitability is investment barriers. It may not be worth it for your competitors to invest in replicating your advantages, especially if your organization has already made a sizable investment and there's not enough demand to support two competitors.

If your organization has an inimitable product, you should focus your attention on maximizing this advantage. In volatile times, organizations with a unique competitive position will be better able to weather the rough spots than their purely imitation-driven rivals. If you don't have an inimitable product, review your CDA to find dimensions where you may be able to develop and offer one.

Match or Beat Where You're Weak

Maybe your offerings are on par with your competitors in some dimensions, but fall behind in others. A short-term strategy may be to meet or beat your competitors in those areas. Of course, doing so over the long term requires substantial operational change. To reduce prices without eroding profitability, for example, requires you to increase the efficiency of your production process. Or, matching the number of competitor locations may require you to invest in expansion. Before you consider going head-to-head with your competitors, ask yourself if you want to invest your valuable resources in a game of catch-up. To quote a little bumper sticker wisdom, unless you're the lead dog, the view never changes. Are you content with that view, or do you want to find a market niche where you can be the lead dog?

Get Out

Suppose you conduct your CDA and find deficiencies that will be difficult or impossible to remediate. You need to ask yourself the difficult question: Is this business model sustainable? If not, get out while you can and reposition yourself where you can fulfill the spirit of your mission, make a unique contribution, and be profitable. Perhaps the most famous example of this strategy occurred when Intel, faced with relentless competition from the Japanese, got out of the dying market for memory chips and began developing processors. The rest, as they say, is history.

As Intel's experience demonstrates, sometimes outpositioning your competition calls for more than a simple adjustment; it may require wholesale reinvention of the organization. As much as your mission drives your strategy, sometimes your competitive position must drive your mission.

Rule 5: Watch Out for Substitutability

Whatever your competitive position, it is no match against the ultimate competitor—progress. The greatest carriage makers of the early 1900s were not destroyed by better carriages, but by automobiles. Record players became antiques not through intense competition among record player manufacturers, but by the invention of CD players.

What revolution will outmode *your* product or service? If you don't know, you should attempt to find out before the marketplace tells you. You may never be able to predict with certainty where the next market shift will occur, but one thing is certain. If you don't seek out and understand the technological and societal trends that impact your business, you will not be able to respond to them proactively. Therefore, high-performing leaders recommend assessing your customers, your competitors, and your organization on a continual basis, in both turbulent and tranquil times.

Case Studies: Bringing the Rules to Life

In other chapters, we profiled high-performing leaders who exemplify the rules we were trying to illuminate. In this chapter, however, because competition is such a multifaceted activity, we're going to focus more on the organization than on any one particular leader. Although competitive position is a function of CEO and senior leader ability, it is also significantly increased when key operational leaders across the organization pursue excellence across the seven dimensions of competition. Here is how that synergy occurs in one of the most important organizations of our times.

Wal-Mart: Always Competitive . . . Always

Wal-Mart founder Sam Walton was almost fanatical about understanding his competition, and the strengths and weaknesses of his own stores. It's part of what helped Wal-Mart to grow, and part of what helps it to continue its success.

To measure customer traffic, Walton would visit the parking lots of K-Mart and Target stores and count the number of cars. At Ames, he would catalog sales prices and measure shelf space allocated for certain items. Walton unabashedly copied the best ideas and practices he found on his reconnaissance runs, including becoming friends with Sol Price of Price Club fame and then adopting his no-frills warehouse retailing concept. One of Walton's most important contributions was to inculcate this attitude in the corporation.

In addition to being a leader in gathering competitive intelligence, Wal-Mart has always been an expert at multidimensional competition. In the cost dimension, Wal-Mart has made heavy investments in information technology to continually drive down the cost of core work processes, thus helping the company to maintain its price advantages. Wal-Mart pioneered the use of UPC scanning for purchases in 1983, two years ahead of K-Mart. A satellite system allows the organization to compile and analyze sales data from all of its stores on a daily basis. Electronic data interchange (EDI) enables Wal-Mart to connect digitally with 3,600 vendors for automated ordering, invoicing, electronic fund transfers, forecasting, planning, replenishing, and shipping. And wide latitude in responsibility allows store managers to set prices consistently lower than their local competitors.

Over the years, Wal-Mart has also continued to increase its product offerings, including an expansion into superstores that sell groceries. Most stores are open extended hours for customer convenience, with many superstores open 24 hours a day. Of course, on the place dimension, the location of these stores has always been one of Wal-Mart's main competitive advantages. By opening its first stores in rural areas that were not served by other large retailers, Wal-Mart obtained first-mover advantage and gained the loyalty of millions of discount shoppers.

Holding all these competitive advantages together is Wal-Mart's unique culture, which involves associates in cost-savings initiatives, and provides stock options and benefits for the majority of employees. Most of Wal-Mart's managers are home-grown, providing employees with high levels of consistency in leadership and corporate values. By respecting employee contributions, Wal-Mart is able to translate employee satisfaction into friendly service, a unique differentiator in the discount retail market.

When you think of Wal-Mart, you probably think of its famous slogan: "Always low prices . . . always." However, as we said throughout the chapter, price is one of the most easily eroded dimensions of competition. To maintain its low-price advantage and ensure its inimitability in this area, Wal-Mart has committed to a rigorous program of assessing its competitors and improving its position on several of the dimensions of competition, including place, offering, and augmentations.

How does all of this position Wal-Mart in a volatile economy? Well, as of the end of 2001, Wal-Mart was still near the top of *Business Week's* "Companies Who Made the Most Money" list. In times of volatility, knowing how to beat your competitors and position yourself to the greatest advantage can mean the difference between market leadership and bankruptcy.

Practical Strategies for Strengthening Your Competitive Position

Wal-Mart is the unquestioned leader in its industry. It has succeeded through a dedication to low prices, high levels of service, great variety, and well-positioned locations. While not everyone will have Wal-Mart's national presence, nor will everyone be vying for the number-one spot on the Fortune 500, Wal-Mart offers a few lessons that are applicable to any organization:

- **Take a multidimensional approach.** Wal-Mart outpositions its competitors in several key competitive dimensions. While many marketing books recommend focusing on one major differentiator (e.g., price or quality), the competitive profile of outstanding organizations is not so simple. High-performing organizations and their leaders obtain advantage in more than one of these key dimensions; the result is a "synergistic kick" that propels the organization to a state of inimitability.

- **Align advantage and practice.** For this synergistic kick to occur, all dimensions must be in alignment. An organization cannot compete on price, for example, without eventually examining its core processes to find new efficiencies. Alternatively, an organization cannot compete on quality and then tolerate unqualified staff or slipshod work. Leaders of highly competitive organizations choose their main source of competitive advantage and then align the entire organization to support it.

A Parting Message: Find Balance in Disequilibrium

We started the chapter with one quote from Andy Grove and we'll end it with another. Grove once said that all organizations go through "strategic inflection points"; these turning points (or disequilibrium phenomena, as they are also known) fundamentally change the competitive landscape. In volatile and chaotic times, inflection points become more common. The spoils go to those who can recognize these trends and capitalize on them before their competitors do.

Being around for such an inflection point is a matter of chance; turning it to your advantage is a matter of skill. Consider the case of Helena Luczywo and Wanda Rapaczynski, two journalists who were working on an underground newspaper at the same time that the waves of democracy began to roll across Poland. These two women rode those waves to found Poland's first independent newspaper. But being first can also mean first to fail. To build on their first-mover advantage, they brought in capital and pursued a careful strategy of investment and expansion, making *Gazeta Wyborcza* the most profitable media franchise in Europe.

Rapaczynski and Luczywo remind us that competition is not first about winning, but about survival. Through competition, organizations survive to fulfill their mission another day. Many of the paper's staff still struggle with the legacy of communism and worry about the need to compete and get ahead. To them, and to us, Rapaczynski offers this advice: "There is only one protection: The best way to keep the devil at the door is to be financially independent. . . . To do good, you must do well." To this, we would add that to do well, you must outposition your competition.

CHAPTER EIGHT

STIR, DON'T SHAKE

The [people] who build the future are [those who] know that greater things are yet to come, and that they themselves will help bring them about. Their minds are illuminated by the blazing sun of hope. They don't stop to doubt. They haven't the time.

—Melvin J. Evans

It's a success most managers would like to claim—leading your team to be best in the world four years out of five. That's the enviable track record of Joe Torre, manager of the New York Yankees since 1995. Under scrutiny from millions, Torre successfully overcomes common leadership challenges—demanding external customers, a difficult boss, and a diverse team of performers—to lead his team to greatness. How he does it provides important lessons for managers who need to motivate their teams in "do or die" situations.

Torre's leadership philosophy could be summed up by Yogi Berra's famous statement: "Baseball is 90% mental—the other half is physical." In a high-pressure situation, an individual's mental state can make the difference between success and failure. Too much stress and a person chokes; too little challenge and he or she under-performs. To help his players walk that fine line, Torre has mastered the art of keeping them motivated, yet relaxed under pressure.

Perhaps Torre's most important leadership technique is to model the behavior he desires. Whatever a player's private turmoil or public challenge, "Joe never panics," as catcher Joe Girardi marvels. Yankees general manager Brian Cashman even has a name for Torre's public displays of composure in difficult circumstances—"calm bombs."

Torre is also famous for "keeping things loose." In shouting matches with George Steinbrenner, he can disarm his notoriously cranky boss with a quick quip. He's learned how to buffer his players from Steinbrenner's criticism, so it doesn't add to their pressure to perform. Once, during a losing streak, he even recommended that the team drink the celebratory champagne *before* a game to loosen them up. Joe Torre demonstrates that leading under pressure means helping your team stay—in the words of James Bond—*stirred, not shaken.*

Of course, we're not saying that leadership in the dugout is exactly the same as leadership in the executive suite. We know that sports metaphors, like battle metaphors, are overused in business literature. However, clichés tend to hang around because they hold a certain truth. Business and sports *do* have several things in common: Tough situations demand that the team win and move forward—or else lose and drop out of the race. Both individual and team performance count. And winners understand the importance of victory without becoming overwhelmed by the possibility of defeat.

Perhaps Warren Bennis, fellow leadership researcher and professor at USC, said it best: "Probably the biggest mistake you can make during any kind of downturn is to choke up. Remember the flying Wallendas? When Karl, the patriarch of the Wallenda family, was in his seventies, he fell 120 feet to his death trying to walk a tight wire. . . . Later, his wife said that before the stunt, for the first time in his life, Karl had seemed concerned about falling. When it came time to perform, he fell because he was focused on not falling, rather than on getting to the other side. In tough times, remember Karl Wallenda. When you concentrate on not losing, rather than winning, you'll find yourself dead on the ground."

Here's how high-performing leaders help their organizations walk the high wire of an uncertain, and often shaky, economy to get to the other side.

Rule 1: Be Vigilant for the Signs of Stress

In volatile and chaotic times, the stakes for performance are higher than ever before. Unfortunately, additional pressure to perform can propel an individual or team that is already anxious into paralyzing fear. In this condition, employees are too distracted to perform their duties well, if at all. Such incidents of "choking" can bring critical projects to a halt. Unfortunately, most managers first notice a choking incident after it has begun to take a toll on the organization. High-performing leaders, on the other hand, proactively seek out and remove these work blockages.

The first step in this process is to be vigilant for the signs of stress. For example, instead of the standard motivational speeches that most coaches use, Joe Torre meets with players in private sessions to identify any problems that might impede their performance. Lina Echevarria, Director of Glass and Glass Ceramics at Corning, Inc., employs the same technique. Her job is to maximize Corning's $2-million-a-day investment in R&D while keeping a team of 45 brilliant, quirky scientists in a creative "zone." She says, "I am always walking into someone's office and saying to that person, 'How does it feel—in this project? In life?' I have this conversation often with people, and not just people whose performance concerns me."

This one-on-one questioning technique enables both information gathering and information sharing. The standard motivational speech, on the other hand, allows only for one-way communication. In motivational speech mode, leaders are unable to gauge how well their employees are holding up under pressure.

Yet this information is precisely what leaders need to know to identify problems and help employees regain their composure and productivity. While inspiring speeches have an important role in volatile times, high-performing leaders know how to balance talking with listening.

The success of the one-on-one interview hinges on the questions leaders ask and how they ask them. Leaders like Joe Torre and Lina Echevarria don't walk up to their employees and bark, "Tell me whether you're about to crack up because I need to know!" Instead, they use an open-ended, compassionate approach. Questions as simple as "How's it going?" or comments like "I know we have some tough deadlines to meet" open the door to a productive dialogue about stress. Not only does such a dialogue help you diagnose stress levels, it also helps you demonstrate empathy for your staff. People are much less likely to succumb to overwhelming anxiety when they understand that stress is a natural reaction to change, and that they won't be punished for feeling or expressing it.

During these one-on-one conversations—and in their daily routine—high-performing leaders stay alert for indicators of individual and team stress. When they start to see an increase in these problems in their organizations, they know that intervention is in order.

Signs of Team Stress (Department-, Division-, or Organization-Wide)

- Low morale
- Increase in sick-day usage
- Increase in complaints or grievances
- Increase in injuries or illnesses
- Increase in turnover

Signs of Individual Stress

- Headaches

- Avoidance
- Difficulty concentrating
- Overreacting
- Short temper
- Depressive mood
- Lackluster performance

Rule 2: Eliminate Stress at the Source

When being vigilant to the signs of stress alerts you to a potential problem, the best way to restore productivity is to remove the source of the stress. Stress at work results from a combination of forces: those that arise in the organization, and those that arise from individual or personal factors. Before you can work with an employee to eliminate a stressful situation, you must first identify the root cause of the problem—organizational or personal.

Sometimes stress in the workplace originates elsewhere. People who bring their personal problems to work with them may require referral to a counselor or your EAP. Others may be unusually susceptible to workplace stress and would benefit from some type of stress-management program. In most cases, however, organizational factors cause or exacerbate stress. In fact, 25 percent of Americans state that their job is the number-one stressor in their lives. The good news is that organizational or job factors are often under your control.

Job stress is often confused with challenge, but these two concepts are not the same. Stress can have an energizing effect in small doses. We all have felt the adrenaline rush that comes from starting a new and challenging project. Challenge motivates us to learn new skills and master our jobs. We feel relaxed and fulfilled when a challenge is met. Thus, challenge is an important ingredient for healthy and productive work.

When does challenge turn into unhealthy stress? When employees are missing one or more of three critical factors in their jobs: *commitment, control,* and *competence.* You'll remember commitment from Chapter 3: Commitment is the extent to which people feel in sync with the organization's spirit and feel encouraged to live that spirit. Control is a measure of whether people feel they can influence schedules, deadlines, performance, work environments, etc. Finally, competence is the state of balance between being bored and underutilized, and feeling underqualified and overtaxed. In other words, reducing the impact of workplace stress means *building a committed culture, giving employees a satisfactory level of control over their work lives*, and *providing them with the appropriate training and job placement to promote a healthy level of challenge.*

Despite leaders' efforts to design the workplace for commitment, control, and competence, stress can still hit. You may have a solid team of people who are performing effectively in their job and who feel committed to their co-workers. Then economic volatility strikes. The company's profits or stock values go down, leadership begins talking about cost cutting, and people start fearing for their jobs. Or you tell them they need to change how they work, and their fear of change causes them to become paralyzed. You can't change the environment in these cases, but you *can* help employees respond to it effectively.

Without your intervention, employees may respond to stress unproductively. They may lose their perspective, become more irrational, and indulge in catastrophic thinking. Such stress-building thoughts ratchet up employees' anxiety levels until they eventually become unable to cope. This, in turn, can lead to such negative outcomes as staff defections, poor customer service, plummeting productivity, and increased worker health costs, among others. High-performing leaders realize that the key to getting employees back on track is by breaking the escalating cycle of anxiety. To do this, they use *behavioral prompts* that remind employees to stop, catch their breath, and regain some perspective. The following four rules describe high-performing leaders' most successful stress-busting strategies.

Rule 3: Launch a Calm Bomb

Like it or not, leading in chaotic times means being in an excruciatingly visible position. Once leaders demonstrate tension or apprehension, it spreads like a virus throughout the organization. Therefore, the more difficult the situation, the greater the need to remain calm. In challenging times, do what Joe Torre does: Launch a calm bomb.

We call this technique centering—the capacity to gain composure both emotionally and physically. When you center, you consciously calm yourself, tune out distractions, and maintain a positive orientation to problems that might make you angry. In our own studies of high-performing leaders, we've found that centering is a vital skill. And it *is* a skill. Centering takes practice because it goes against a natural tendency to express or project anger and tension.

Centering is the "method acting" approach to leadership: Act calm when you don't feel that way, and if you do it enough times, you'll find that your mental state mimics your behavior. Simon Walker, whom we'll learn more about in the next chapter, calls this technique "making tea." Walker, who is executive director of a British yachting business, honed his leadership skills during dangerous races. His strategy was to deflect crew attention from the perils of the sea by maintaining a veneer of calm. "During a crisis, my third command was always to put on the kettle," he explains. "By demanding cups of tea for the whole crew, I got one person out of my hair, and I introduced a normalizing factor into a crisis situation. If the skipper wants a cup of tea, it can't be that bad."

Rule 4: Remember the Jambalaya

Here's one final sports metaphor. It's the big game. Nine seconds are left on the clock. You have one timeout remaining. Your quarterback is about to run the final play, hopefully for the game-winning touchdown. He's high-strung; in fact, he's been throwing up with fear before every game. You call a timeout, beckon your quarterback over, and say, "Didn't you like the jambalaya?"

At least, that's what Al Pacino's character did in the movie *Any Given Sunday*. Talking privately with his quarterback, the coach says, "Remember when you came to my house for dinner? You didn't eat the jambalaya I made. Didn't you like it?" The quarterback smiles, replies (in censored form), "No, it was terrible. Why do you think I've been throwing up all season?" and then goes back to win the game.

How many other coaches—and leaders—in a similar situation would have sharply reminded their player of the importance of the game? But like all great leaders, Al Pacino's character understood that *star players know exactly what's at stake*. To remind them in a negative or threatening way can create unbearable pressure that can compromise their performance. Reinforcing an obvious challenge also implies that you question your employee's intelligence, which punctures that person's self-confidence and concentration. Negative reminders create negative expectations: "I expect that you don't understand the importance of this, and I expect that you might fail."

In the face of a challenge, the worst thing you can do is say, "Don't choke." It's the equivalent of calling out to Karl Wallenda on the high wire and saying, "There's no safety net. You'll die if you fail. Don't look down." When you frame a challenge in terms of failure, failure is what you get. If employees succeed despite your "encouragement," you will have an even bigger motivational challenge next time because of your perceived lack of trust.

In contrast, Pacino's character's coaching strategy was brilliant in two critical ways. First, it broke the cycle of anxiety, enabling his quarterback to forget about the pressure to perform just long enough to calm down and focus. Second, it established a personal commitment. It reminded the quarterback of the respect and friendship that framed their working relationship, effectively saying, "I will support you, no matter what happens." So when your team is facing a defining moment, remember the jambalaya.

Rule 5: Make Time for Humor and Play

Humor is one of the best methods for defusing stress. Research tells us that when we laugh, we pump our bodies full of endorphins that generate feelings of euphoria and actually strengthen our immune system. Both emotionally and physically, having fun helps people stay resilient in the face of challenges. Not only does humor make it possible to get through the challenge of the moment, it also helps create the bonds of commitment that strengthen a team for the next challenge. Therefore, high-performing leaders remind their teams to take challenges seriously, but never to take themselves too seriously. When they sense that a choking incident is about to occur, they often use humor and play to break the cycle of anxiety.

Nancy Deibler manages Sprint's small-business sales division in Kansas City, Missouri. Long-distance telephone sales is a job low on commitment, control, and challenge—lots of restrictions, cold calling, and tedious repetition. Most operations of this type experience high rates of turnover, but not Deibler's. She is able to keep people stirred, not shaken by building fun into the workday. When things get too tense, Deibler closes the office at 3:00 P.M. and everyone goes bowling. Or she goes to a baseball game, has a cookout, sings karaoke, makes up goofy sports contests, dresses up in costumes . . . . whatever helps them blow off steam. Deibler understands that some of these activities may seem hokey to outsiders, but she really doesn't care. "It lifts productivity," she says, along with staff morale and retention.

Bringing humor to the workplace is now a multimillion- dollar consulting business. But it needn't be an expensive proposition. The best humor is always spontaneous. As Deibler does, look to your employees for cues that it's time for fun and then let them take the lead.

Rule 6: Give It Some Distance

Sometimes an office under pressure starts to look like Grandma's house on Thanksgiving weekend. Voices raise, tears flow, and doors slam, simply because too many people have experienced too much togetherness for too long. It's not that people necessarily dislike their jobs or their co-workers; it's just that a team can only take so much of the same stimulation.

Of course, all teams go through a rocky stage. Team theorists have even given it a name—storming. You may recall that storming comes after forming and before norming and performing. However, there is a difference between productive storming and "choking." When a team is storming, the members actively engage each other in debate that, even though heated, leads to solutions. When a team is choking, the members will avoid the main topic, refusing to interact, acting with hostility, or getting sidetracked with irrelevancies.

When a team starts to choke, it's best to give it some distance. You can try throwing a party or some other fun activity. But certain members of your team may have reached the point where they don't even want to socialize with each other. If timelines allow it, give everyone a break. Call a moratorium on team meetings or give everyone a day or two off to regroup.

When you lead a team, you're not immune to the pressures of too much togetherness. At times, every leader becomes too tired, angry, or anxious to remember the jambalaya. When that occurs, even the mildest-mannered leader can become something that rhymes with "brass pole." It's OK to give *yourself* a timeout. When you do, remind the team that you're taking a break from the situation, not from your commitment to them. Use phrases like, "You know what? I'm tired and starting to lose focus. I know we're all really committed to working this out, but I need to take a break. How about you? Let's talk about this again on Monday." The more you role model these behaviors for your staff, the more they will emulate them, and incidents of choking will decrease.

Case Studies: Bringing the Rules to Life

The two leaders we've chosen to profile in this chapter provide the perfect cocktail for helping your organization stay "stirred, not shaken" in volatile times. In the first of our two case studies, we'll see how an executive used the tools of calm, humor, and distancing to inspire his staff to a breakthrough solution for falling revenues. The second story shows how another leader used a little jambalaya to help his organization overcome a very public financial, customer service, and public relations crisis.

Donald Winkler and Ford Motor Credit Company: Breakthrough Leadership

Unfairly or not, accountants don't exactly have a reputation for being cut-ups. Donald Winkler, Chairman and CEO of Ford Motor Credit Company, is the exception to the rule. Staffers anxiously await his Cato attacks (from the manic Cato in the *Pink Panther* series of movies), when he calls people unexpectedly and asks them to rattle off their strategic priorities. Winkler has resorted to paying sullen employees to ask questions at team meetings in morale-challenged situations. And one of his favorite management tools is a red latex clown nose.

Call him a little outrageous. Call him Patch Adams for the finance set. Just don't call him if you want the standard approach to leadership. Winkler preaches what he calls "breakthrough leadership," the creation of opportunities for finding transforming solutions. To illustrate his style, let's examine a town hall meeting that Winkler conducted in 2000.

Ford Credit (the financing division) and Ford Motor (the manufacturing division) were experiencing a downturn in revenue from declining car sales and a declining share of the financing for those sales. Winkler invited a team to an off-site retreat to develop a solution. Staffers arrived expecting the usual drill: solemn discussions punctuated by the requisite team-building exercises. Instead, they found a party.

Over the doorway to the meeting room hung a banner that said, "Congratulations. 2002 reunion." As staff members entered, Winkler shook their hands and congratulated them—and gave them noisemakers and hats so they could celebrate. Lloyd Hansen, controller for Ford Motor Company North America, explains Winkler's strategy. "This was a reunion, for two years from now, and we were celebrating our success. Then we starting talking to each other about what we had accomplished. And, of course, that led to ideas about what we really wanted to accomplish."

Out of that party grew some very serious changes. The team agreed to radically simplify a lease-pricing schedule that had been confusing to both customers and dealers. It also simplified categories of customer creditworthiness, another complicating factor in the lease process. Most important, they decided to change the formula for calculating lease residual values, allowing for lower monthly lease payments. Yes, Ford Credit would take a lower margin, but the plan would allow Ford to sell more cars, which would, in turn, increase volume for Ford Credit.

Energized by the party, the team put the plan into effect, much of it within 48 hours. Ford Motor sales shot up immediately, and Ford Credit was financing a higher percentage of those sales, up 10 percent from the year before. Directly due to these innovations, Ford's operating profits in the first half of 2000 rose 17 percent over the previous year.

When you look at Donald Winkler, you need to look past the clown nose. Winkler's secret weapon is not just his silliness, but his ability to turn expectations on their head and get employees thinking in new and creative ways. When he saw Ford's falling profits, he could have—as many leaders do—ordered his team on a course of action, or brought the team together, set some doomsday scenarios, and then commanded them not to screw up. Instead, he gave them an opportunity to calm down, loosen up, and exchange ideas in a setting that was conducive to breakthrough thinking.

J. Brendan Ryan, FCB Worldwide and the Biggest Client Defection Ever

J. Brendan Ryan had the dubious distinction of witnessing the largest client defection in the history of advertising. His company,

FCB Worldwide, had handled the advertising for the Chrysler and Jeep arms of Chrysler for 20 years. A rival ad agency, BBD&O, had handled the Dodge advertising business. In 2000, Chrysler, which was seeking cost-savings in its advertising budget, asked the two agencies to recommend some strategies. BBD&O suggested that using one advertising agency would streamline the process and drive down costs. FCB thought Chrysler would be better served with a diversified and specialized approach, while still being able to hold down costs. Chrysler disagreed, and FCB lost the account—all *one billion dollars* of it.

In addition to this major loss of revenue, FCB faced the potential of more client defections. Clients are exceptionally fickle in the advertising world. "Losing a high-profile account has the potential to plant doubt in the minds of other clients, both existing ones and those in the process of deciding to work with you," says Ryan.

No one would have blamed Ryan and FCB if they had choked. Instead, they rallied to preserve their existing clients, sign new ones, and end the year with an 11-percent increase in billings. Ryan's strategy was to key into the resilience of his employees through the new economy equivalent of a staff meeting—the global employee memo. In fact, Ryan is rather famous for his staff memos. Colorful, earthy, impassioned, and inspiring, they are not your standard missives from the CEO.

When the bad news hit, Ryan let the news sink in over the weekend so he could center himself before communicating with employees. Then he began his memo by acknowledging his personal disappointment with the decision and letting employees know that it was okay to vent their anger and disappointment, as well. His next move was to praise the team responsible for the pitch to Chrysler. "Having been in that room, [I know] that damn pitch was superb," Ryan told everyone in the company. What an extraordinary reversal of expectations it must have been for that team to lose a billion-dollar contract and receive public praise for doing a great job.

Then Ryan moved on to remind people of FCB's bright future—the quality of their people, the clients they had already signed, and the clients that were waiting to be signed. It was the most successful memo Ryan had ever written. More than ten times the normal number of staff responded; the vast majority favorably.

There's a fine line in dealing with setbacks, Ryan explains in characteristic Ryan style. "Some companies say, 'Oh, well it wasn't our fault. We did everything perfect. And, oh, it doesn't matter anyway. We're just fine.' Bull ****. People aren't that stupid. If they hear those things, they'll say that you're idiots. You've got to 'fess up that the setback was a kick in the chops. But at the same time, you can't accept that the setback happened because your team is a bunch of blockheads."

J. Brendan Ryan is a great example of how a leader can "rush to think" even in the midst of a crisis, and then create a strategy that takes an organization to new heights of success. After centering himself, Ryan engaged his team in an empathic discussion of the situation. By expressing his own disappointment, Ryan let his staff know that it was okay for them to express theirs. However, he also reminded them that the key to success is to acknowledge and learn from setbacks, and then move forward. Rather than let his team get mired in negativity, Ryan provided the positive framework they needed to avoid choking and keep achieving.

Practical Strategies for Stirring, Not Shaking

Both of these leaders know how to stir their teams to greatness in the face of a challenge. By reversing the status quo and facing adversity with a positive outlook, both Ryan and Winkler were able to tap into the creative energy of their teams to develop solutions that would not have been possible through ordinary means. Here are some of their tips so you can do the same.

- **Remember that being a little hokey is not a crime.** When some people at Ford hear Winkler say things like, "Turn that paradigm upside-down," they probably want to roll their eyes. But you can't argue with a 17-percent increase in profit. Or, in Deibler's case, with an industry-leading retention rate. Sure, people will groan a little bit at first. At least if they're groaning, they're not choking. Of course, each leader must find the mix of inspiration and hokey-ness that he or she is comfortable with. And that takes us to our second lesson . . .

- **Be authentic.** Joe Torre speaks to employees individually, Winkler holds town meetings, while Ryan uses global e-mail. Torre is a figure of calm. Winkler cavorts in a clown nose. Ryan swears like a truck driver. Each approach is correct because it works for that specific team and situation. Most important, it is an authentic expression of the leader's style. When applying the rules, be yourself and let your employees respond accordingly. There's nothing less funny than forced hilarity, or less relaxing than mandatory recreation.
- **Yes, there is an "I" in team.** High-performing leaders recognize that teams are greater than the sum of their parts. Paradoxically, they also recognize that teams cannot function without individual performers. Therefore, high-performing leaders first treat stress as an individual problem, reducing the risk of contamination to the team. Even leaders with senior-level responsibilities use one-on-one interviewing and coaching to proactively seek out problems and inspire great individual performances.

A Parting Message: Remember the Jambalaya

To summarize the lessons of the chapter, we can return to Rule #4: Remember the jambalaya. It's not a bad metaphor for managing people in high-pressure situations. Jambalaya is comfort food, meant to fill people both physically and emotionally. It is also a mix of ingredients. Each piece is unique, yet all add to the whole. No two people make jambalaya in exactly the same way. It is supposed to be improvisational, fun, and more than a little spicy. So, too, is leadership in a turbulent economy. We hope the lessons and tools provided in this chapter will help you devise your own mix of ingredients to keep your team "stirred, not shaken."

CHAPTER NINE

CUT THROUGH THE NOISE

On the field of battle . . . the spoken word does not carry far enough . . . . Gongs and drums, banners and flags, are means whereby the ears and eyes of the host may be focused on one particular point.

—Sun-Tzu
The Art of War

In 1987, DuPont plant manager Dick Knowles reluctantly accepted a transfer to a struggling ammonia plant in Belle, West Virginia. When Knowles walked in the door, the plant was being besieged from within and without. Plant facilities and equipment had decayed to the point of being unsafe. Workers were angry and distrustful of management. On one hand, the community was terrified that an industrial accident might wipe out the town. On the other, they worried that DuPont would close the plant, leaving 1,000 people out of jobs. In the midst of all this hubbub, some managers were literally at each other's throat.

Eight years later, when Knowles walked out the door for another assignment, injury rates were down by 95 percent, environmental emissions were down by 87 percent, productivity had increased by 45 percent, earnings per employee had tripled, and the changes in morale were immeasurable. Knowles's strategy for success was to develop a vision of mutual respect and openness, then take it to the front-line workers, take it to the streets, and repeat it ad nauseum until even the most skeptical became believers.

He describes this process in his own words: "I decided my first objective would be to meet everyone, every single person in the plant. . . . You do that by walking around, just talking to people, listening to them; that way you tap into the life of an organization. I did that for five hours a day, every day, and I continued doing it throughout my eight years there. . . . We used to have business meetings twice a week, out in the plant, in the laboratory, the control rooms, the shops, all over the place. . . . I made a priority of inviting people to visit the plant and see what we were struggling with. . . . At one point we had 500 people a month visiting the plant. . . . It worked the other way, too, because I spent a lot of time in the community, as much as 40 percent of my time, just talking to people."

Despite Knowles's modesty, what he did was more than walking around and "just talking to people." He actually cut through the chaos and tensions—the "noise"— surrounding a difficult situation, to reach all stakeholders with a message that harnessed their commitment for a better future.

Unfortunately, you don't need to face the challenges that Knowles did to feel that you're under siege. Large and rapid swings in the business environment have created a global economic battleground, with millions of organizations scrambling for competitive advantage. As Sun-Tzu reminds us, in the heat of battle, the field becomes so noisy and confusing that messages have difficulty getting through.

Without the ability to communicate effectively in times of chaos, a leader's other skills are worthless. If you can't communicate, you can't achieve, outposition your competitors, partner with customers, build a culture of commitment, or cut costs while protecting value. To put it bluntly, everything you've learned in your career and in this book could be wasted if you can't get your message through.

Because communication is so critical, the noise that obstructs communication can be the greatest threat to a leader's success. Therefore, high-performing leaders like Knowles use "gongs and drums, banners and flags" to cut through the noise and reach their troops with clear and compelling messages. These rules will show you how to do the same.

Rule 1: Diagnose the Noise

To get your message through to your stakeholders, you first need to diagnose the barriers to communication. Scientists who study electronic communications have identified five major types of noise that impede the flow of information. These same types of noise play themselves out in interpersonal and organizational communications, and are the major sources of conflict and misunderstanding in human relationships. Once you understand these five types of noise, you will be able to diagnose the communication roadblocks you face and implement the strategies in this chapter to overcome them.

Resistance

Resistance noise is signal distortion—the difference between what leaders *think* they said, and what their audiences actually heard. We've all had this experience. You believe you've communicated a message clearly, only to find that the person on the receiving end misunderstood your intention or just didn't get what you said.

The root cause of resistance is individual differences in the way people communicate with one another. Neurological research tells us there are four major ways that people process information; each of these relationship styles determines individual communication preferences and styles. When a person of one style doesn't tune in to another person's style, the potential for miscommunication skyrockets. Because every organization includes people of all four styles, leaders must learn how to tune in to each type to get their messages across. In the next section, we'll discover how high-performing leaders reach their audience by crafting messages that meet diverse communication needs and expectations.

Interference

If resistance is "I just don't get it," then interference is "I don't *want* to get it, nor do I want you to get it." Interference is an act of communication sabotage—someone deliberately trying to prevent your message from getting through. Examples include an office rival disrupting a meeting, people "forgetting" to pass along important information, and outright defiance.

Interference is a manifestation of someone trying to wield power and control over you, and in volatile and chaotic times it can be an especially difficult problem. People like to feel they have some level of control over their lives. As life gets more unpredictable, people become confused and frightened, and they try to bring some sort of order back into their lives by whatever means they have at their disposal. When stakeholders are committed to the organization, they try to assert control by helping the organization adapt to the changing environment. Those who are not committed to the organization will wield their power to promote their self-interest over the interests of the whole. In turbulent times, high-performing leaders stay on the alert for signs of interference and either redirect the energy of interferers into more productive channels or, in extreme cases, separate them from the organization.

Attenuation

Attenuation is the "fading out" of a signal. If you've ever felt that your messages just disappear somewhere in the corporate bureaucracy, then you understand what a threat attenuation can be to your ability to communicate. By the time information gets from leadership to front-line workers, it often gets filtered through so many layers that the original message isn't "strong enough" to get through.

While attenuation is sometimes a problem of geography—people are simply too far apart—it is more often a problem of complexity. Think of a tightly coiled ball of wire. While the two ends may be only a few inches apart, the pathway between them may be dozens of feet long. The pathway of communication in an organization is sometimes like that. Another department may be on the same floor as yours, but for purposes of communication they might as well be on Mars. High-performing leaders learn how to cut through the complexity to deliver their message directly to the people who need to hear it.

Cross-Talk

Have you ever tried to concentrate when two, three, four, or more people around you are all trying to talk at the same time? This phenomenon is called cross-talk, and in the days of party lines it happened on phone conversations all the time. Today's organizations often seem like one big party line, with different teams quickly moving in different directions, and everyone talking at once. At any given moment, a leader's message has to compete for attention with all these other conversations going on in your organization. To strengthen the signal strength of their message and prevent it from getting lost in the "background roar," high-performing leaders learn how to simplify, amplify, and clarify their messages.

Glitches

Glitches are unexpected crises that knock communications off track. Unlike the previous four types of noise, which have clearly definable causes, glitches seem to come out of nowhere. No matter how well you have planned for turbulent times, you can expect that a glitch will eventually happen—and the higher the other forms of noise, the more likely a glitch will happen. Glitches are unexpected only in the sense that you never know exactly when they are going to hit. Therefore, successful leaders prepare for glitches by developing contingency plans so they can take quick and appropriate action when a crisis does hit.

High-performing leaders use these definitions, or ones similar, to diagnose the types of noise occurring in their organizations and then react appropriately. In volatile and chaotic times, all five types of noise are likely to be occurring simultaneously, requiring a protocol for noise management that addresses them all at once. The next set of five rules show you how to implement this protocol so you, too, can get your message through.

Rule 2: Tune In

A key to communicating during volatile times is preventing resistance. Above all, you must ensure that your message gets through clearly to everyone who needs to hear it. When the people receiving your message misunderstand your intentions or just don't get what you're saying, the results can be disastrous. Misunderstandings between managers and front-line staff have led to the departure of the most talented employees, labor campaigns, strikes, and more. Misunderstandings between businesses and suppliers have ended formerly-healthy partnerships and crippled entire supply chains. Misunderstandings between executives and their boards have ended many a CEO's career. Especially in volatile times, avoiding the resistance that can cause these communication breakdowns is essential to a leader's survival. This is why, as we said earlier, high-performing leaders go to great lengths to key into their organization's diverse communication needs.

More than 30 years of neurological research shows that individuals tend to receive and process communications in one of four distinct ways. These four basic communication styles are the *intuitive, rational, personal*, and *functional communicators*. Each of us gravitates toward one of these ways of communicating, although most people display a mix of styles. We develop these styles through a complex mix of heredity, nurturing, and education.

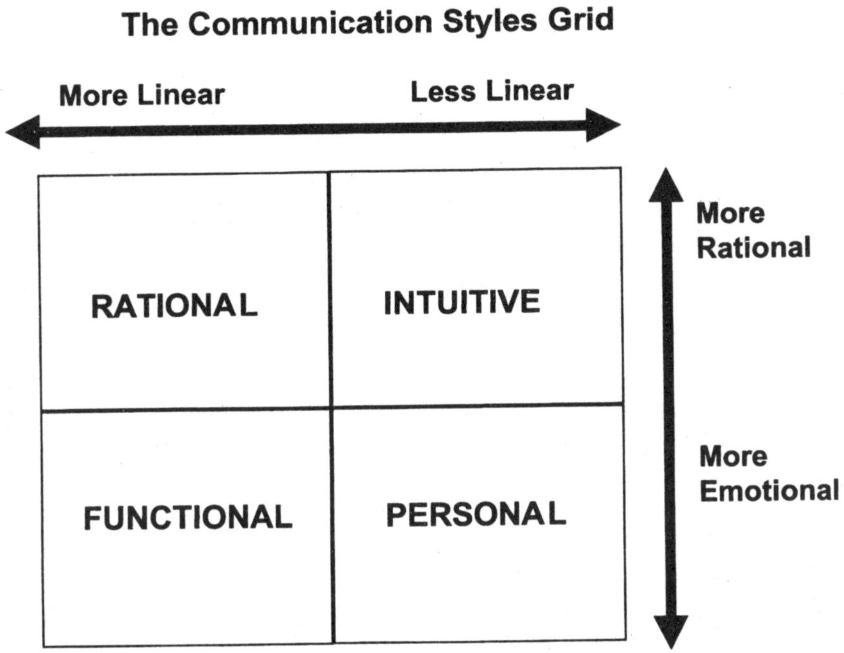

The above figure shows how the four main types of communication styles arise from relative degrees of linear and rational thinking.

Rational Communicators

Rational communicators are structured, rational, analytical, and data-driven. They value facts, technical expertise, and systematic methods for getting things done. Therefore, the best way to get a message through to a rational communicator is to use data and logical arguments.

Functional Communicators

Functional communicators are structured and emotional. They value planning, decisive action, and tangible and immediate results. Be direct, down-to-earth, and practical with functional communicators. Answer the question: How can we get the job done?

Intuitive Communicators

Intuitive communicators are nonlinear and rational. They focus on the big picture or vision of the future, rather than the here-and-now. They place a high value on concepts, imagination, and creativity. When dealing with intuitive communicators, it's best to talk in terms of strategy and innovation.

Personal Communicators

Personal communicators are nonlinear and emotional. They are often dynamic, friendly, and charming, valuing empathy, sensitivity, and the opportunity to work with others. Focus on the human side of an issue when dealing with personal relators.

An effective leadership message is one that includes four subtle variations on the same message—one each for rational, functional, intuitive, and personal communicators. We call this style M-Pathic, short for the ability to empathize with all types of people and communicate along multiple paths.

Ineffective leaders focus on just one communication style, typically their own. For example, if you give a "just the facts, ma'am" presentation, everyone but rational communicators will tune you out. On the other hand, once you give people something to hang their hat on, they'll be more open to considering other points of view. If you take your rational message and add a functional piece (e.g., "The data says that we should do X, Y, and Z this year, and Tina's team will be in charge of that") functional communicators will pay attention to the data because the practical message grabbed their attention. Add a personal message (e.g., "I understand that might make us uncomfortable . . .") and an intuitive message, (e.g., "but it will help us serve our customers better, become more innovative, and thus ensure a more competitive position"), and you have the entire audience tuned in.

Mary Brown, President and CEO at Ochsner Foundation Hospital in New Orleans used this four-pronged approach to communication when she held town hall meetings for all employees. To remain competitive in a volatile healthcare market, the executive team and board had decided to radically reorganize its structure. To explain the need for the change, Brown cited data (rational) from several assessments that had been conducted on quality, competitive, financial, and cultural issues. Then she empathized (personal) with the feelings that everyone shared, most notably the fear of change. Third, she addressed functional concerns about who was going to do what by when. Finally, she keyed into the intuitive aspects of the audience by talking about long-range visions and strategies for success. By tuning in to the four communication needs, Brown was able to quickly rally her staff for a significant change effort.

Rule 3: Tune Out—Or Take Out

As we said earlier, interference is the equivalent of a guerilla attack on a leader's attempts to communicate. It's a safe bet that during times of volatility and uncertainty, some people are not going to like the actions you're taking, especially if those actions involve doing something other than what you've always done in the past. Change can be difficult for some people, especially when the outcome is unknown. Unfortunately, uncertain outcomes are a fact of life in turbulent times, and the people who have a great deal of difficulty with this are likely to lash out and attempt to sabotage your efforts. The great risk of this interference is that not only can they damage your personal effectiveness as a leader, but they can also derail all of your plans and projects. Assuming that your plans and projects will offer significant benefit, this interference can jeopardize the whole organization's chances for success.

It's pretty easy to distinguish interference from a simple misunderstanding or constructive criticism. The tip-off? You detect ill-will from the other person, either veiled or in-your-face. In other words, if you think someone is conspiring against you, you're probably right. As the old saying goes, "Just because you're paranoid doesn't mean they're not out to get you."

All forms of interference are motivated by a dysfunctional and self-centered need to wield power and control. How interference is expressed, however, depends on the personal characteristics of the person who is doing the interfering. In interference, as in much of life, people tend to play to their strengths. Therefore, rational communicators will tend to use data to contradict your messages, while personal communicators may attempt to manipulate you emotionally to get what they want. Functional communicators will use policies and procedures to block your communications, while intuitive communicators may dismiss the creativity or scope of your thinking.

It is useful to understand the motivation of interferers so you can recognize them—preferably before they launch a full-blown attack on you. For practical purposes, a single, core methodology applies to all of them. After all, whatever their personal motivation, if you let interferers block your communication, the result is the same. Your message gets blocked and your plans can fail. Even when they can't stymie your efforts, interferers will steal the time and energy that would be better spent serving your organization and its customers. In many organizations, interferers are the classic case of the squeaky wheels that get the grease.

In very mild cases, high-performing leaders deal with interference by tuning out instead of *tuning in*. For example, you might ignore isolated cases of whining or diplomatically avoid someone who is being manipulative. This is often the most expedient approach when volatile times demand your full attention and the interferer is not disruptive to the rest of the team. Behavioral research supports this approach; ignoring inappropriate behavior tends to help the perpetrator extinguish it on his or her own.

In some cases, however, an effective leader must deal with interferers by surgically "taking 'em out." Of course, we're not talking about a Sopranos'-style solution here. What we do advocate is defusing their arguments and separating interferers from their colleagues so their negativity does not contaminate the rest of the team.

Use this three-part strategy to take out interferers. First, separate ego from issue. React to an incidence of interference in a way that respects the person and his or her position, yet makes it perfectly clear that the behavior is unacceptable in terms of the interests of the organization. Begin by saying "I understand" and then repeating the concern. So, for example, if you have a functional relator who is afraid of change, you might say, "I understand your concern that we've never done things this way before, and that we don't have a procedure for this yet." Or, in the case of a personal relator who is trying to manipulate your emotions: "I understand that you are concerned there might be personal risk here. . . ." Second, follow with a rational and functional statement: "However, the results of our research say that we need to get the following done . . ." Third, conclude with a visionary statement that tunes into the intuitive aspect of the person or group: "and if we don't, we won't be able to fulfill our mission." "I understand, however, because"are the three core elements to dealing with any interferer.

What happens if the interferer won't let up? At that point, you should repeat the essential message with one important addition. Begin with "As I said," then repeat, "I understand . . . however, we have this responsibility and we must get the following done, because . . ." What if this second response doesn't work, and someone persists with interference until it becomes defiance? Follow with this line: "But, it appears that you are not understanding my message. This is becoming disruptive to the team. You and I need to meet privately to talk about this issue. I don't believe it's productive for us to continue in this fashion."

Interference Script
I understand . . .
However, . . .
Because . . .
For Defiance Mode:
But, . . .

The most important thing to remember when dealing with interference is that you are the protector of the customer and those that serve the customer. Interference is more than an attack against you as a person; it is an attack against the organization's ability to serve. As a guardian, steward, and servant, you cannot let that happen.

If this approach seems a bit stern, you're right. Virtually every solution we have offered in this book is driven by collaboration and commitment. However, when an individual or group lacks the willingness to collaborate and commit, then it's time for you to either rechannel the behavior or remove the threat. Defiance is an extreme behavior that requires clear consequences, up to and including separating the person from the organization.

In today's business environment, such forthright action is particularly important. An increasingly prevalent and alarming type of extreme interference is violence in the workplace. Violence typically erupts when the defiant party is subject to intense stress in some aspect of his or her life other than work. If you sense that one of your employees is on the verge of violence, be sure to call for assistance immediately from HR, your EAP professionals, or external professionals. At any time, if you believe someone is capable of violence, do not meet with that person alone.

Rule 4: Cut Through

As we said in our definition of attenuation, isolation and complexity are two of the most common sources of communication problems in organizations. Leaders often become trapped in the chain of command, not realizing that the usual trickle-down method of communication can isolate them and impede the flow of information. When that happens, a leader must bypass the bureaucracy to go *directly* to the people. General Patton did it by flying to the front lines and conducting tank traffic himself. Mother Teresa did it by bypassing the hierarchy of the church and going to the streets to be with the people of Calcutta. You'll have to decide what "cutting-through" means in your organization.

An excellent example of cutting-through is Wendel Province, CEO of Midas, Inc. When Province was appointed chief executive in 1998, the organization was mired in an unusual growth scheme. Midas had opened company-owned Muffler and Brake shops in direct competition with shops owned by franchisees—some even on the same street. Franchise owners were in an uproar and profits were dwindling.

Province, whose motto is "Life isn't about contracts, it's about trust," cut through the noise and turned Midas's culture on its head. As one of his first acts as CEO, Province met with individual shop owners to reaffirm his commitment to them. He then promptly sold off the company stores and sent each franchise a share of the profits. His next act was to promise each Midas franchise owner a discount on a different part per month, enabling them to boost sales by offering monthly specials. Province then cemented his relationship with franchise owners by covering the cost of a national television ad campaign. In bypassing the ordinary chain of command, Province was able to forge relationships with the people who really drive his organization's success.

Rule 5: Stay on Message

In volatile times, it's not enough to take your message to the farthest reaches of the organization—you must also ensure that it stands out from all the rest. If not, your message can get lost in all the cross-talk going on around it. To overcome the confusion inherent in volatile times, you must continually strengthen your message through consistency, repetition, clarification, and simplification.

A less-than-stellar turnaround at Sears illustrates what can happen when leaders don't stay on message. In 1990, the retail chain was at the tail end of a five-year slump and had just been accused of fraudulent business practices in its Sears auto centers. These problems were complicated by a significant decline in the morale of its more than 300,000 employees. To turn things around, CEO Arthur Martinez assembled the "Phoenix" team (as in rising up from the ashes). One team developed and launched a series of town hall meetings designed to inspire and energize employees. However, here is where Stephen Kearns, director of the project, admits "we dropped the ball on this one."

Although the town hall meetings were somewhat successful, they were not as successful as they could have been because the executive team did not stay on the message of participation-driven change. The executive team and regional managers received extensive training with a consistent message. However, the district managers, who were supposed to conduct meetings for store managers, were poorly prepared and uncommitted to the town hall concept. Six months into the project, participation fell to 30 percent. At the same time, Martinez's two top executives, who had not been supportive of the initiative, began rigorous cost-cutting without employee input and, therefore, diminished the goodwill that Sears had worked so hard to obtain. In both word and deed, Sears executives cut into the success of their turnaround by not sending a consistent message.

Rule 6: Practice Rapid Response Communication

Glitches seem to strike without warning. The reality, however, is that leaders often fail to recognize when conditions are ripe for a glitch and act proactively. Especially in volatile and chaotic times, leaders must remember that glitches will occur, even in the most effective organizations. How does this happen? Volatility causes the other four forms of noise to increase, which makes communication in all of its forms more difficult. In turn, an increased level of communication problems can lead to a breakdown somewhere in the system. When that crisis occurs, rapid and appropriate response is the key. However, to be able to respond rapidly, leaders must have planned ahead and established clear guidelines for communication and action. Here are some battle-tested guidelines for glitch management.

Be Open and Compassionate

In organizations, glitches usually take the form of a financial, operational, legal, or public relations crisis. Some examples include environmental disasters, product recalls, and incidents of malpractice or wrongdoing. Whatever the circumstance, stakeholders will place some blame on the organization and its leadership—usually with good reason. High-performing leaders quickly accept responsibility for any part their organizations may have played in the crisis. They do not deny or hide the truth. Instead of first focusing on how to protect the company, they focus on protecting its customers with compassion and honesty.

Partner with the Public

High-performing leaders never assume they know what the public needs during a crisis. Instead, they assign key team members to partner with the public to find answers to the following questions: What does the public want to know? What information and services will help restore their faith and goodwill in the organization?

Partner with Trustworthy Sources

If an organization has experienced a significant drop in credibility due to a crisis, benchmark leaders call in objective third parties to mediate the crisis. For example, food or drug manufacturers may request additional oversight from the FDA during a product recall. Or organizations suspected of financial sleight-of-hand might immediately call in an independent auditor. By aligning themselves with organizations that are above reproach, or at least removed from the crisis, leaders demonstrate that they are genuinely interested in bringing the situation to a just conclusion.

Partner with the Media

When the media becomes involved in a crisis, many organizations unwisely treat them as adversaries. Benchmark leaders, on the other hand, partner with the media to share information with their customers. This may be difficult to do, particularly if you've had negative experiences with the media in the past. Nevertheless, you cannot change the fact that the media have a job to do, and they *will* do it by finding a story. The question becomes: Which story will they tell? To present their organizations in the best light, leaders must partner with the media to develop accurate and favorable media coverage.

To consider how well these rules help organizations through crises, compare the strategies of Johnson & Johnson during the Tylenol scare in the 1980s and the recent Ford and Firestone escapade with SUV tires. Johnson & Johnson followed these rules and overcame what could have been a potentially fatal blow to customer trust. As of this writing, Ford and Firestone are still weathering the negative effects of their "head in the sand" approach to crisis management.

Case Studies: Bringing the Rules to Life

As a follow-up to our discussion of communication during crisis, let us begin with the case study of Odwalla, a company that overcame a major legal, financial, and public relations glitch with an effective communication plan. Then we'll recap the main points of the chapter by reviewing how a hospital CEO made extensive use of "gongs and drums, banners and flags" to revive a failing organization.

Stephen Williamson and Odwalla: Life-or-Death Decisions

The spirit of Odwalla, the natural juice company, is best captured by its origins. In 1980, in Santa Cruz, California, its founder began squeezing fresh orange juice and selling it out of the back of a 1968 Volkswagen van. Founder Greg Steltenpohl built the company on a platform of absolute freshness; for the next 16 years, juices were left unpasteurized to retain their just-from-nature taste. To preserve product quality and safety, the company relied on its fruit growers to comply with its stringent standards for fruit handling. Then in 1996, the company experienced the first major glitch in its history.

One of their suppliers had failed to follow the standards, contaminating a batch of apple juice and unleashing a deadly strain of *E. coli* in Washington state. Dozens of people fell ill and one toddler died. At the time, CEO Stephen Williamson almost wished that the company would die, too. He recalls, "Our vision statement is about nourishing the body whole, yet people were getting sick from our product. Then a little girl named Anna died from our apple juice, and Odwalla's world changed forever."

Williamson recognized that the noise surrounding the crisis was escalating at a level that would destabilize the whole company. His first move was to reassign managers to one of three teams: managing the existing business; plotting a reemergence strategy; and managing inquiries from the health department, media, and customers. He also ordered a complete and immediate recall of all products, which ultimately cost $6.5 million. He explains, "We had no crisis-management procedure in place, so I followed our vision statement and our core values of honesty, integrity, and sustainability. Our number-one concern was for the safety and well-being of our customers."

Nevertheless, Odwalla faced an immense challenge. Sales plummeted 90 percent and the stock price fell 34 percent. Customers filed more than 20 personal-injury lawsuits, and a grand-jury investigation pitted key employees against one another in an effort to assign blame; several of Odwalla's core employees quit under the pressure from this external interference.

Williamson and his team managed to bring the company out of the crisis through a strategy of rapid response communication with all stakeholders. "At first, things were changing so quickly that the core management team met every 15 minutes. As things calmed down, we began meeting once an hour, then twice a day, and finally once a day. As the pace of information changed, we changed how we communicated," Williamson says.

He instituted regular company-wide conference calls to tune in and update employees about the crisis, staying on message with each group of employees. Odwalla also turned to its route managers to cut through layers of bureaucracy and personally visit retailers each day to give information about the situation. While more expensive than a third-party distribution system, Odwalla's route management system helped cut through the noise and more than paid for itself during the crisis. Willamson explains, "Following the recall announcement, we had only a few days to reassure our trade partners and our consumers. In less than a week, our coolers would have been unplugged, our products thrown out, and our space in the market lost."

To reduce the risk of attenuation with its customers, Odwalla expanded its open-door policy with the general consuming public. It bought ads in all the local papers to alert customers to the recall and offered to reimburse medical expenses for anyone who was injured by its juice. To prevent cross-talk, Odwalla was completely open about the grand-jury investigation, pleading guilty to federal criminal charges and paying a $1.5-million fine. They publicly acknowledged that their previous "never pasteurize" policy was a mistake, invested in a $1.5-million system for flash pasteurizing its juice, and consented to rigorous oversight from the FDA.

Today, the company is again profitable and growing. Williamson attributes this success directly to his company's ability to cut through the noise and reconnect with the people essential to its success. "Odwalla didn't survive by accident. For 15 years, we built a reservoir of goodwill. When crisis struck, some of that goodwill drained away, but a lot of people still believed in Odwalla, largely because we never deceived or manipulated them. When things go bad, people want to look inside a company and see whether its soul is good. Ours is."

Although Odwalla had no formal glitch-management plan, it demonstrated rapid response communications in its immediate recall of contaminated juice and redeployment of management teams. It also demonstrated how to cut through the noise on all levels and stay on message. Throughout the E. coli crisis, Williamson and the leadership team reduced attenuation by reaching out to front-line staff, retailers, and customers, even going so far as to visit stores and speak personally with their customers. They also reduced cross-talk and resistance by staying on message throughout the crisis, delivering well-crafted messages that captured the special vision and values of its corporate history. Williamson and his team demonstrated how leaders can pull an organization back from the edge of disaster by knowing how to diagnose and manage noise.

Patricia Dorris and Palo Pinto Hospital: Calling All Stakeholders

Patricia Dorris, CEO of Palo Pinto Hospital in Texas, is a communicator in the Sun-Tzu class. In 1999, her small 99-bed county hospital was struggling, like most other healthcare providers, due to the Balanced Budget Act's reduction in Medicare and Medicaid reimbursements. In fact, the tiny hospital had a huge financial drain, losing nearly $300,000 a month. The Board decided that new leadership was in order, and promoted Dorris from Patient Services Administrator to interim CEO (now her permanent title).

Dorris knew that a unified effort was necessary, so she employed all the "gongs, whistles, and banners" at her disposal to get stakeholders on board with the turnaround effort. First, she created a team of board members, physicians, and managers to develop a strategic plan for the organization. In fact, it was the first time that the entire organization had worked on a single strategic plan. Dorris then rolled out the plan with physicians and employees, asking them to collect ideas for implementation. Concurrent to this effort, Dorris met with community leaders to educate them about the impact of the BBA on their hospital. Her diligent advocacy eventually resulted in the community rallying around the hospital to vote in a tax increase to keep the hospital alive.

Dorris contacted executives from financially successful hospitals and emulated their best practices. She also reached out directly to help patients and physicians remain in the community. Before her tenure, many physicians were leaving for jobs in larger cities, and too many patients were following them for care. To stem this outgoing tide, she established physician and patient forums to explore specific needs and "tune-in." This resulted in new physician retention and recruitment programs that overcame resistance and redirected energy from interference into the turnaround plan.

Recognizing that the efforts of one person are not enough, Dorris made communication a core part of the culture at Palo Pinto. Each day, employees rotate onto customer satisfaction teams, where they cut through the barriers to patient service by speaking directly with a certain number of patients, staff, and physicians, and then reporting on their levels of satisfaction. Leaders then aggregate these results to drive improvement efforts.

By cutting through the noise and involving all stakeholders in finding solutions, Dorris and her team implemented several important cost-cutting and revenue-enhancing programs, which took the hospital from a $2.2-million loss in one year to a $2.3-million profit in the next.

Just as Odwalla's story demonstrates the last three rules particularly well, Dorris' story highlights the first two: *tune in* and *tune out—or take out*. First, Dorris tuned into the needs of each stakeholder group: helping the community understand the need to support the hospital, helping physicians see why they needed to stay in the community, and helping employees see why patient satisfaction was so critical. With each group, Dorris integrated the rational, functional, personal, and intuitive aspects of her message to inspire everyone to action. Along the way, she encountered interference from those who were afraid of change or who wanted to preserve their self-interest over the good of the hospital. Dorris overcame these incidents by getting everyone focused on the reality facing the hospital and the actions needed to make that reality a more prosperous one.

Practical Strategies for Cutting Through the Noise

As we observed successful leaders in action, we discovered that they had developed common strategies for cutting through the noise to get their messages across, regardless of the circumstances. Here are some tactics that any leader can use to be a more effective communicator in tumultuous times.

- **Use the write stuff.** Regardless of your ultimate medium of expression (a speech, e-mail, or a face-to-face conversation), benchmark leaders advocate writing out a script beforehand. Leadership communication is too important to leave to chance, and you never know when a stray comment will spark an episode of resistance or interference. Even if they only have five minutes before a meeting, benchmark leaders will pause to think and write out key points that tune in and stay on message.
- **Be aware of implicit messages.** High-performing leaders plan their communications carefully because they realize that stakeholders dissect every leadership word and dig for a deeper message. Everything a leader writes, says, or does is a form of communication, even if it's not a speech or memo. Staff surveys are a form of communication; so is one's choice of artwork or the configuration of one's office. In fact, scientists who study communication tell us that only 40 percent of communication is content; 60 percent is context. For that reason, successful leaders consider the context of their message as well as its meaning.

A Parting Message: You Can Only Compete Through Your Crew

Simon Walker is Managing Director of Challenge Business, a British company that manages the logistics for the world's most challenging yacht races. Perhaps the most difficult is the BT Global Challenge, a grueling 30,000-mile race around the globe backwards—that is, against prevailing winds and currents. To make things a little more interesting, each yacht is manned by a crew of amateur sailors who have never worked together before. Skippering a yacht under such conditions can teach anyone the leadership communication skills needed for success.

Walker recalls his 1996 stint as captain of the *Toshiba Wave Warrior*. "I can only compete through my crew," he explains. "So first I had to learn each crewmember's agenda. One guy wanted to win at all costs. Another guy wanted simply to make it around the world. The key was to avoid agreeing to the lowest common denominator." So Walker devised a communication strategy for each crewmember's agenda. By using "gongs and drums" with one group and "banners and flags" with another, Walker was able to take his team from different starting points to a shared victory at the finish line.

Walker's advice applies to the world outside of yachting, too: Every leader is only as competitive as his or her crew. The best leaders give their teams the edge through an ongoing dialogue that enables the achievement of shared goals—a dialogue that always begins by tuning in to the needs of your "crew." In this way, leaders live out Malcolm Forbes's famous epigram: "If you want understanding, try giving some."

CHAPTER TEN

FOCUS OR FAIL

No horse gets anywhere until he is harnessed.
No steam or gas ever drives anything until it is confined.
No Niagara is ever turned into light and power until it is channeled.
No life ever grows great until it is focused, dedicated, disciplined.

—Dr. Henry Emerson Fosdick

Today, software runs everything from your car to your refrigerator. One would think that something so important would be reliable, but of course that's not true. Software is highly susceptible to error—just count the number of times your computer crashes or your Web browser goes off-line. And if your organization pays for software development, you know that it often comes in over budget and past deadline, with a few bugs thrown in at no extra charge.

So, how would you feel if you were an astronaut on the space shuttle, and you knew that your life was in the hands of the programmers who developed the software that runs the mission? Surprisingly, you would feel completely confident.

The "on-board shuttle group," a branch of Lockheed Martin, develops the software that runs the space shuttle. A team of about 260 men and women, the shuttle group is one of just four organizations worldwide to win the highest ranking from the federal government's Software Engineering Institute (SEI). In fact, the SEI based its standards partially on the work of the group. How good *is* this team? Their software has never crashed and is completely bug-free. In the last three versions of the program, each one with 420,000 lines of code, only three minor errors occurred. In the business world, a similarly complex program would have about 5,000 errors. How do they do it?

One important factor in their success is knowledge of the stakes. With each shuttle launch, the software controls $4 billion in equipment, the lives of the astronauts, and the reputation of the space program. A tiny error that wouldn't even be noticed in another application could put the shuttle miles off course or cause a dangerous accident. In fact, the group's senior technical manager must fly from Houston to Florida before each launch to certify that the software will not endanger the shuttle and its crew. As one engineer points out, "If the software isn't perfect, some of the people we come to meetings with might die."

Even more important to the group's success, however, is the highly focused process they use to develop the software. With the Lockheed Martin group, about one-third of the software-development process occurs before the first line of code is written. At the start of a new project, NASA and the programmers sit down together, block out the specifications for the new program, and then write them out in minute detail. Once they lay the blueprint, nothing is changed without consensus from both sides. The process is so critical that they have teams dedicated to double-checking and documenting the process. Because of this "process behind the process," the team has developed an annotated history of the code and an error database. Together, these databases help continuously improve the quality of the outcome and simplify the process of developing future programs.

In addition to producing results that are as near to perfection as humanly possible, the process also promotes a corporate culture unique to software developers. When you walk through the offices of the on-board shuttle group, you might be surprised to see a pretty normal-looking bunch of people. No Gen-X software gurus with grungy jeans and bleary eyes—just professionals with steady 8-to-5 schedules and lives outside the office. Because the team uses the process to focus so intensely and plan out projects in the smallest detail, they rarely have an occasion for late nights or last-minute crunches.

John Munson, a professor of computer science at the University of Idaho, says, "Most people choose to spend the money at the wrong end of the process. In the modern software environment, 80 percent of the cost of software is spent after the first version of the software is written. Because the programmers don't get it right the first time, they have to spend lots of time and money fixing and redoing it. But in the shuttle group, they do it right the first time. And they don't change the software without changing the blueprint. That's why their software is so perfect."

No one ever said that leadership was rocket science. But the stakes are nearly as high and the margin of error almost as narrow. In turbulent times, leaders must "do it right the first time"—they must focus, or fail.

In the previous chapters we've discussed the challenges that require your attention in turbulent and chaotic times: cutting costs, building commitment, maximizing knowledge, reducing stress, partnering with customers, etc. How do you integrate and balance all of these priorities? How do you know the right thing to do—and when to do it? How do you stay focused when everything around you is changing? And how do you generate near-perfect results without killing yourself or your team? For leaders, as for the on-board shuttle group, the answer is to *follow a focusing process.*

As we watched our high-performing leadership group in action, we found that they tended to approach challenges in similar ways. To manage the complexity that surrounded them, these leaders used a five-step focusing process to simplify and clarify their responsibilities. This process provided enough structure to guide the organization through volatile times, yet enough flexibility to enable customized and creative solutions. The process was not always linear; sometimes the leaders found themselves going back to a previous step or doing two steps concurrently as needed. But for the most part, high-performing leaders followed these five steps in this order.

Rule 1: Define the Challenge

As we noted in Chapter 1, leaders cannot follow the "ready, fire, aim" school of leadership and expect to hit their targets. To aim well and quickly, they must, of course, have some idea of their target. Most leaders set these targets through some sort of goal-setting or strategic-planning process. Unfortunately, goal setting in the absence of the right information is an exercise in futility. Even the noblest goals are unattainable if internal resources are not available to fulfill them, or if trends in the external environment point to another direction entirely. To establish and meet goals for their organization, leaders must consider—and often refine—those objectives in the context of the challenges they face.

High-performing leaders approach challenges with one simple credo: If you don't know what the problem is, you can't fix it. Therefore, the first thing they do in any situation is *define the challenge*. Especially in a downturn, leaders consider the trends in their business environment—looking out for the next 6, 12, and 18 months—to identify the nature, scope, duration, and causes of any likely challenges.

Identification of the problem, while a critical first step, is not enough; the organization must be able to find and mobilize the right resources to solve it. Therefore, high-performing leaders also *measure the organization's readiness to meet the challenge* by conducting formal assessments of the areas we've discussed in the previous chapters: competitive position, financial health, the state of customer partnerships, etc.

In conducting these assessments, high-performing leaders practice what we call strategic humility, the recognition that one person does not have enough information about the challenge to make good decisions. They involve all stakeholders—anyone who might have knowledge of the challenge—in measuring its parameters. Stakeholder involvement provides the best data for decision-making, because it gathers information from those who are closest to the work and to customers. It also helps stakeholders recognize and accept the need for change, thus simplifying implementation.

In 1994, Unilever Chairman Niall FitzGerald discovered the importance of strategic humility in defining the challenge. At that time, FitzGerald headed Unilever's British soap division, where one of his principal responsibilities was the launch of a powerful new laundry detergent with extra scrubbing chemicals. In fact, the new detergent was so powerful that it ate right through clothes—and made Unilever a laughingstock in the British press.

FitzGerald called a meeting with 30 Unilever executives to resolve the crisis. At one point, he stopped the meeting and asked how many people in the room did their own laundry. He was amazed to find that not one person raised a hand. "There we were, trying to figure out why customers wouldn't buy our soap—and we didn't even know the first thing about how it was used," he says.

That was the last time FitzGerald relied solely on the input of a management team to make important leadership decisions. Since the detergent fiasco, Unilever has established policies that improve partnerships with employees and customers, including a residency program in developing countries where new recruits become immersed in the culture by living with a local family. These policies provide the organization with real-time information on impending challenges and its readiness to meet them.

Rule 2: Establish a Vision for Meeting the Challenge

After defining the challenge, leaders establish a vision for meeting it. This vision serves two purposes. First, it provides a concrete direction for the organization. Second, it provides inspiration and creates a community dedicated to success. Dee Hock, visionary founder of VISA, says, "Far better than a precise plan is a clear sense of direction and compelling beliefs. Unless we can define a purpose for this organization that we can all believe in, we might as well go home. . . . Next, you're going to have to agree on a set of principles for the organization. . . . What we're trying to do is build a community. And it's only when that community has solid agreement on purposes and principles that you can start talking about the concept and structure of the organization."

To establish their vision, high-performing leaders conduct a gap analysis; that is, they consider the challenge at hand vis-à-vis the organizational capacity to meet it. The resulting gaps highlight immediate priorities for action. So, for example, one organization may face a significant financial crisis that could necessitate a reduction in force. In another situation, the challenge may be to outposition competitors by providing an innovative product or service. In that case, a gap analysis may reveal that the organization will have to invest in personnel, knowledge assets, and research and development.

In today's fast-paced economy, many opportunities present themselves at once. In fact, it would be unusual if your gap analysis revealed only one problem. Therefore, you need to decide which opportunities will provide the greatest benefit for your organization and its customers. In this step, as with the rest of the process, high-performing leaders rely on data rather than their own biases. Instead of jumping to conclusions, selecting a pet project, or working where they're comfortable, leaders will consider every opportunity that arises.

To ensure that they are conserving the organization's resources by focusing on areas of significance, high-performing leaders conduct a cost-benefit analysis for each opportunity. They analyze each option in terms of its costs and benefits—the cost of time, equipment, and personnel required to act on the opportunity versus the benefits for cost reduction and value preservation, customer partnerships, knowledge assets, etc.

If this sounds like a lot of data analysis, you're right—it is. Like the process used by the shuttle engineers, the process used by high-performing leaders involves a lot of work before the "work" begins. It is also unforgiving of sloppy information. As any software engineer will tell you—garbage in, garbage out.

Even the most brilliant visions are worthless if they don't go through this cost-benefit analysis. Just ask Kevin Ulmer. In 1987, Ulmer watched carefully as the government launched the Human Genome Project. He knew that whoever was first to decode the human genome could make millions, if not billions, in the pharmaceutical industry. He also knew that the government was not exactly a fast mover. So he came up with a brilliant idea: Start his own human genome project and beat the government to the jackpot. However, Ulmer decided to develop his own gene sequencers, rather than use off-the-shelf technology, believing his methodology would be more efficient. While Ulmer spent months trying to perfect his sequencers, his rivals used existing sequencers to leapfrog ahead of him. Consequently, Ulmer's company lagged behind while his competitors were first to get venture capital, first to market, and first to make hundreds of millions of dollars. The outcome might have been different if Ulmer had considered the costs and benefits of each approach before dedicating himself to one.

Rule 3:
Plan to Leverage High-Impact Opportunities

After selecting the opportunities with the most benefit to the organization, high-performing leaders create a plan to address them. As in the first step, leaders recognize the limits of their own information and experience. Turbulent times usually demand organization-wide changes, often on several fronts at once. The magnitude of this challenge requires the in-depth operational knowledge and contribution of those affected by the changes. Therefore, leaders assign a cross-functional team of experts to deal with each initiative, share the data from the initial assessment, establish goals and expectations, and then work with the teams to develop plans.

Because so much work has gone into the front end of the process, the planning step is straightforward. It involves deciding who should do what, where, and when. To ensure that planning activities stay on track, high-performing leaders build the five-step process into team expectations, so team leaders can use the process to stay focused.

In today's economy, planning is more important than ever before, as the recent tech bust proves. HelloAsia.com has used the power of planning to avoid dot-com disaster and tap into a powerful global market. The number of subscribers to online services in Asia is growing by 80 percent a year; by the end of 2002, more than 50 million people will be on-line. HelloAsia.com offers free e-mail service to subscribers, who are then enticed to the sites of its Asian corporate partners. In return, subscribers receive reward points that they can redeem at on-line merchants. Since its launch in 1999, the company has enrolled more than 500,000 subscribers and nearly 100 corporate partners.

The key to HelloAsia's rapid growth and survival has been translating the company's vision into a formal plan. "A lot of start-ups think they're too dynamic to plan," says founder Henry Ellenbogen, who launched HelloAsia with Harvard Business School classmate Chih Cheung, now the company's CEO. "They say, 'We're growing too fast to follow a plan.' But we didn't feel that we had a choice." HelloAsia takes the start-up energy and enthusiasm of its staff and channels it into a meticulously crafted process that breaks every project into components. The team then assigns each component to teams and asks them to meet the needs of their service region. Says Ellenbogen: "On the one hand, you need clear, functional goals with precise guidelines. On the other, you need local implementation, which means empowering people at a local level." Senior leadership regularly interacts with staff to ensure they understand how their pieces fit into the whole, and they monitor progress to ensure teams stay on task and on target.

With empowerment comes some limitations, however. At the start of each new project, the leadership teams work with employees to ensure that both parties understand what falls within the scope of a role and what doesn't. Within their roles, employees have freedom to find creative solutions to problems. At the same time, fixed role definitions clarify expectations, ensure that "the right person is in the right place," and keep everyone focused. Cheung explains, "All of our people are overachievers. Their natural tendency is to try to do whatever needs to be done, regardless of whose job it is. . . . Sure, we're decentralized, empowered, and all that. But we're trying to build an extremely complicated business, and without a central plan . . . we'd be running amok."

Rule 4: Practice Rolling Implementation

Because so much data analysis and planning goes into the process before implementation begins, projects led by high-performing leaders have a high success rate. Of course, any initiative, no matter how well-planned and well-led, is bound to hit some rough patches. High-performing leaders proactively avoid these problems by setting clear expectations, defining responsibilities, monitoring the team's progress closely, and holding teams accountable for performance.

IBM uses these management techniques in a process they call rolling implementation. In 1998, Sandra Morris, Vice President of Finance and Enterprise Services and Director of E-Business at Intel, used rolling implementation to meet a significant challenge: In six months, develop a Web-based ordering system that would handle $1 billion in annual sales. Not only did Morris and her team make the deadline, they also met the $1-billion sales goal within 15 days of launch. They met their challenge by following a structured process that held managers accountable for their piece of the plan and intervened swiftly whenever they encountered a speedbump. Morris believes that this seemingly rigid protocol is actually the key to making a large company move quickly and smoothly.

To make rolling implementation happen, Morris practiced constant managerial oversight and communication, adjusting short- and long-term goals quickly as necessary. The centerpiece of this strategy was the "program office"—a "nerve center" that planned the project in detail, assigned roles, and ensured that groups communicate with one another. The outcome was, as Morris describes it: "What the people in the trenches were doing lined up with the executive vision. . . . These are huge, complex products and everyone has to understand what's going on to keep them moving forward."

A commitment to cross-functional communication and teamwork was also critical to the success of rolling implementation at IBM. In many high-tech companies, implementation falters because of the barriers between externally-focused sales and marketing departments and internally-focused engineering departments. Intel's program office broke down these barriers by assigning interdisciplinary teams to the e-commerce initiative. The open exchange of ideas that occurred within this interdisciplinary setting produced the most effective solution in a tight timeframe.

Rule 5: Test, Refine, and Repeat

Despite the effectiveness of the process, high-performing leaders understand that one round of problem solving rarely addresses every challenge, especially in volatile times. And while you're off addressing one set of challenges, the next set has been creeping up on you. Therefore, the true test of a leader's commitment is not whether you implement the plan the first time; but whether you are willing to test, refine, and repeat the process in a continuous cycle of improvement. Like the software engineers in the on-board shuttle group, high-performing leaders use the process time after time to upgrade both their outcomes and the methods they use to generate those outcomes.

Capital One has used this scientific approach to leadership to outposition and outperform its competitors. Spun off from Signet bank in 1994, Capital One is now one of the ten largest credit card issuers in the United States. Its founders had little experience in banking, but revolutionized the industry by dreaming up the "teaser rate" card and the "balance transfer" option. Those two innovations aside, the true secret of Capital One's success has been a commitment to continually testing and adjusting its strategy. "For every action we've taken," says Jim Donehey, Capital One's CIO, "we know what the reaction has been. If we sent out a blue envelope and a white envelope, we know which envelope went to which customer—and we've recorded what the reaction was in each case."

Adds Nigel Morris, President: "Very few companies have the ability to test and learn." This commitment to testing and learning is what differentiates Capital One from the rest of the banking industry. The company collects data and tests its efficacy in every area of operations, from product development to customer service to hiring and retention. In one year, the company conducts more than 28,000 experiments involving new advertising approaches, new markets, and new business models.

"Credit cards aren't banking—they're information," explains Rich Fairbank, Chairman and CEO. "When we started this company, we saw two revolutionary opportunities: We could use scientific methodology to help us make decisions, and we could use information technology to help us provide mass customization." As a result, it can deliver customized offerings to its customers—more than 6,000 kinds of credit cards to date. "What we've done," says Fairbank, "is to create an innovation machine."

Case Studies: Bringing the Rules to Life

In this section, we have selected three case studies instead of our usual two to demonstrate how the five-step focusing process can be used in any industry and at any state of an organization's existence. We begin with the story of a team of leaders who used the process to launch a successful technology start-up. Then we include a study on how the process, used repeatedly, has helped a hospital survive and thrive in the volatile healthcare market. We conclude with an example of how one manager used the process to mobilize a global workforce in a large organization facing significant challenges.

Critical Devices, Inc: Focus Is Critical

Jay Lopez, Principal of LJBB Enterprises, approached Chairman Leo Lopez (who, incidentally, is his father) with an exciting new discovery. Andrew Levi, President of technology service provider Aztec Systems, had made an important technological breakthrough. Soon after the three men met to discuss the possibilities of the new product, they launched Critical Devices, Inc. (CDI), which is setting a new standard for integrated IT performance monitoring and inventory management.

The story began when Levi and his team at Aztec began looking for an off-the-shelf solution to a customer need. Customers had been asking for a relationship-based model for performance monitoring and inventory tracking, but no one offered a product that provided all the required solutions in one cost-effective package. So Levi wrote some specifications for the ideal product and asked his developers to build a prototype. In 30 days, they came back with a working model. That offering now provides corporations around the world the ability to identify, inventory, monitor, track, and manage any IT device throughout its life cycle. Levi says, "We recognized very early on that we were really on to something here. Every other 'Aztec system' in the world needed the ability to create sticky relationships with the companies they serve."

There was just one "problem"—the idea was almost *too* good. The vision of bringing relationship-based IT services across industries, devices, and product life cycles was a compelling one. However, the company began to pursue those markets without a strong marketing focus. Jay Lopez describes the situation, "We weren't going after the low hanging fruit in the IT world. . . . We were trying to get into too many markets at the same time." Because Critical Devices had an unfocused strategy, it really had no strategy.

Like many technology start-ups, the company had become enthralled with the possibilities. Now they needed to focus to bring those possibilities to life. Leo Lopez explains, "Critical Devices is so applicable to so many businesses that we became euphoric. . . . I think that the testament to the company is at some point we recognized that you can't possibly go after all of the vertical markets that are out there. We needed to focus. We had to make it successful beyond any reasonable doubt in one vertical market and let other markets take care of themselves."

To *define the challenge* they faced, CDI partnered with customers using what they call the "ladder effect" of adoption. They started with smaller service providers, who were more open to discussions with a new company. Using those first few customers as references, they were able to access medium service providers, then large service providers, then OEMs. Levi says, "We went to the market and we really tried to listen to them . . . and understand what they thought they were trying to accomplish over time."

Based on this information, Critical Devices *established a new vision*—to offer relationship-based, integrated services to the IT market *first*, and then build out from there. Their strategy was to get to the market early and get as many clients signed up as quickly as possible. In fact, Critical Devices's early financial model called for signing up 100 service providers every year, with each service provider then bringing in 200 devices per month over time. Based on this vision, Critical Devices *created a plan*, which included direct-mail campaigns and other mass-marketing activities, and then *implemented it*. To *test and refine their strategy*, CDI ran financial algorithms and soon found that there might be a better way.

Based on their modeling data, CDI decided to take an even more focused approach: The company would target very large service providers that could bring in 100,000 devices each year. Levi adds, "We also changed the way that we found the partners and what our internal processes became in order to support them. If you are only signing up 12 to 15 service providers a year, then you are not doing any direct-mail campaigns and you're not using traditional advertising campaigns—you are using a relationship-based approach."

The new strategy brought some early wins in the first part of 2000, which snowballed after the late-year economic downturn, as service providers became acutely aware of the need to reduce expenses. Within the first six months of 2001, Critical Devices has exceeded its sales targets and is successfully signing on some of the largest IT service providers in the world. Despite a volatile and chaotic economy, and the special threats inherent in any Internet-based start-up, Critical Devices is succeeding because of its commitment to a focused process for leadership.

Hamot Health Foundation: A Focus on Healing

For John Malone, CEO of the Hamot Health Foundation in Erie, Pennsylvania, the arrival of healthcare reform in the 1990s created a challenging new business environment: Proposed changes in healthcare financing would reduce the hospital's revenues by over $40 million in less than three years. For Malone and his stakeholder partners on the board, medical staff, and management team, only two choices seemed viable: Take charge of the situation or quit the business.

Malone chose the former option, and began establishing a context for action by *defining the challenges* threatening the organization. Only he and a few members of the board and executive team grasped the full potential impact of the challenge. Unless he shared this knowledge, and did so quickly, he risked losing the trust and, ultimately, the willingness of stakeholders to accept massive change. To reach as many stakeholders as possible as quickly as possible, Malone "multi-pathed" his message, convening town hall meetings of all employees and physician stakeholders, speaking with local civic and business organizations, writing op-ed pieces, and holding special briefings for the press. In every communication, Malone stayed on message by defining the challenge in concrete terms: Hamot must reduce expenses and/or increase revenues by $40 million.

Malone knew that the challenge of healthcare reform would require much more than the mere reduction of headcount and costs; it would demand the comprehensive restructuring and redesign of work systems at every level of the entire organization. To accomplish this Herculean task, he knew he must win the full support of the only people who possessed the knowledge and skill necessary to do it—the physicians and staff who delivered care. He proposed a *vision for meeting the challenge*, one of customer-focused restructuring through a process of collaborative work redesign. This vision of invited every stakeholder in the organization to participate in a comprehensive assessment of the organization's mission performance and to become involved in making it better. As Malone said, "It is not a vision for the meek of heart, but one that honors each stakeholder with opportunity to participate in his or her own survival."

To guide the implementation of this vision, Malone and his team developed a core set of values that would guide the process and serve for identifying opportunities and establishing priorities for action. These values would drive the assessment of the organization's challenges and establish priorities for restructuring, including work redesign and workforce reduction if necessary.

Malone followed up on the town hall meetings by engaging all 3,000-plus employees, a sample of several thousand patients, the board, the community, and the entire medical staff in a comprehensive assessment of work focus: "Are the right people, in the right place, at the right time, for the right reason and cost for quality?" That question became a mantra for reform for the internal consulting teams of managers, physicians, and front-line employees at Hamot who guided the change process and worked directly with stakeholders to collect work data. These teams then benchmarked the data assessment against a national healthcare "best practices" database to identify risks and opportunities for action.

Ultimately, the benchmark analysis revealed that Hamot needed to remove over 27 percent of the operational costs that were weighing down the organization and preventing it from focusing its energies on patient service. Working with an internal team of consultants, Malone shared this diagnosis with all stakeholders, through the same multi-path communication method he had used to launch the undertaking. He recruited new leaders such as Dr. James Pepicello, former Chair of Surgery, as COO, and repositioned others to new roles, including moving Vice President Don Inderlied from human resources to strategic analysis and improvement. They, in turn, formed internal consulting teams and evaluated the opportunities against Hamot's vision to determine which opportunities offered the greatest promise. Based on these results, they *developed and implemented plans* to accelerate change in key areas—scheduling, the role of management, professional role responsibilities and skills mix, and consolidating and streamlining overlapping departmental functions.

After implementation, Malone and his team *tested the efficacy of his vision and plan* by conducting a reassessment of the mission and work focus, as well as the organization's financial health. As the change program moved into its second year, results exceeded expectations: Hamot achieved more than $15 million in savings the first year alone. And while necessary workforce reductions occurred initially, fully two-thirds of the savings came about as a result of team-driven work redesign, which increased the organization's capacity to serve more patients while sustaining and, in most cases, improving the clinical quality of care.

In the years since that first challenge, Hamot has used the process on a continuous basis, most recently to implement a new organizational model that advances the role of physician executive leadership even further. The results include a dramatic increase in market share, profitability, and—most importantly—quality of service, which has led to national recognition as a top 100 hospital.

Rita Garcia and Xerox: As Common as Possible, as Different as Necessary

Rita Garcia is Vice President of Customer Service Operations for Developing Markets at Xerox. In essence, Garcia is responsible for customer service in 127 countries outside of the U.S., Canada, and Western Europe. When she was brought in to fill this role, her goal was to develop profitable revenue in developing markets for Xerox, a former technology icon struggling to regain its preeminence.

To *define the challenge* she faced, Garcia and her team asked customers about the commonality of their experience. For example, did Ford Motor customers in Argentina have the same experience as those in Detroit? Unfortunately, the answer was often "no"—for reasons that were as varied and complex as the countries Xerox serves.

Of course, providing service in 127 different countries is intrinsically complex because of cultural, political, and technical infrastructure issues. However, these problems were magnified by Xerox's own internal complexities. Operationally, Xerox provided customer service via three different routes: employees, subcontractors, and distributors. Directives to service directors in developing countries were handed down through Xerox's hierarchy with little thought to national or regional needs. Garcia says, "The way they [service directors] learned about the business and the way Xerox wanted it executed was almost like the game 'telephone.'" Market research in North America would design the service specifications and send them through organizational channels to service directors. These directors, in turn, would customize the specifications based on national and cultural differences in technology infrastructure, human resource infrastructure, and other factors. This inconsistency among practices raised operating costs and fragmented the quality of customer service. It was a case of too little sensitivity on one hand and too much customization on the other.

Intriguingly, Garcia found that despite national differences, customer needs were similar all over the world. After all, a broken copier in Brazil needed the same parts and service as one in Turkey. Therefore, the challenge became to create a seamless global customer-service brand that would still respect cultural differences. Garcia *established a vision to meet this challenge*: "As common as possible, as different as necessary."

To implement that vision, Garcia met with service directors, beginning with Eastern Hemisphere directors, then Western Hemisphere, and finally bringing all service directors together in a summit in Brazil. Garcia told the directors, "Our responsibility is to function as a global network of global resources and to do business in the best interest of Xerox's customers." She explained that Xerox and many other companies were doing business as multinational companies but were calling themselves global. That is, they would "push" a North American solution on developing countries—which would then try to customize the product to specific interests—rather than engage customers in developing one truly global solution. Based on this new understanding of what it means to be part of a global company, the team crafted a vision statement: "The quality of the service brand is the global benchmark in the industry that compels customers to overwhelmingly choose Xerox."

During the seven-day meeting in Brazil, service directors shared the unique challenges of doing business in their respective countries. Talking about these differences helped the team drill down into the commonalities. As the team members talked about their contributions, they also developed a global knowledge-management network so everyone knew who to call regarding different types of problems.

As a result of these global team meetings, service directors and Garcia identified six strategic initiatives designed to establish that global service benchmark and, not coincidentally, improve the health of Xerox as a company overall. The focus of the initiatives were customer satisfaction, service revenue, creating a competitive advantage, growing the customer base, distinguishing service models by business segment, and deploying technology to increase profitability and service quality.

In developing these strategies and obtaining employee participation, Garcia used a *planning process* that was as global as the team's vision. One of Garcia's employees, stationed in India, would craft a draft of a strategy and then send if off for comment. As

Garcia explains, "The guy in India would write and then the guy in Turkey would comment. Then it would move to Brazil, then to Argentina, then to Mexico . . . . then it would go to Hong Kong and China. By our midnight it would be morning in India and start to be reworked again." By "following the sun," the global team accomplished in 24 hours what a domestic "9-to-5" team would have taken weeks to finish.

To keep this diverse team on track, Garcia developed a highly structured *rolling implementation process.* Each team would receive a calendar showing what was happening each day, and what was on the agenda for that day. Garcia met with the team via teleconference each month to monitor what each team was doing, share progress, and promote knowledge exchange. Each month, team members were asked to rate their progress as "red, yellow, or green," with green meaning "go." By publicly sharing their progress, employees began to take responsibility for their part of the plan and to help others "go green." Through this consistent process of sharing information, the team became a cohesive whole. Garcia explains, "All of a sudden they were not customer service of Hong Kong or customer service of Mumbai. They were customer service of Xerox. . . . It was terrific. I got 100-percent participation. People would call on their vacations because they wanted to know. The art of leadership is to engage people in a way that creates an understanding of their own importance to the whole."

Testing the results has revealed a dramatic improvement in customer satisfaction and profitability in developing-country operations, an important step on Xerox's road to recovery. The key to Garcia's success has been a focusing process that harnesses the rich and diverse contributions of a global team while managing the risks of confusion and chaos inherent in such diversity and geographic dispersion.

As Garcia says, "To manage diversity, you must have a process." As the world moves to an increasingly global business model, and as businesses within the United States increase the diversity of their workforce, leaders need to find a model for leadership that is as "common as possible, as different as necessary." The best way to accomplish that goal is through a process that provides a common ground for employees to work together, yet respects differences and enables teams to develop flexible, customized solutions.

Practical Strategies for Focusing

Although the rules provide a detailed overview of the five-step process, a review of our case studies yields some additional practical techniques for focusing in volatile times:

- **Follow the sun.** Just because we present the process as five linear steps does not mean that progress must occur in a purely linear fashion. High-performing leaders find innovative techniques, like following the sun, global teams, and "customer ladders," that jump-start team progress and create synergy among the players. These multi-tasking techniques make it possible for an organization to create, implement, and test plans along multiple tracks and concurrent timelines.
- **Define the role of leadership.** As carefully as high-performing leaders set expectations and define roles for teams, they also set clear boundaries for leadership. To ensure that the process works, leaders must practice both hands-on and hands-off management. To help the organization stay focused, leaders must monitor the process, provide visible leadership, and intervene when things go off track. At the same time, leaders must include stakeholders in gathering, analyzing, and applying data if they want to create solutions greater than the management team could have created alone.
- **Create a protocol for sharing information.** Information is both the fuel and the lubricant of the process. Data helps leaders understand the challenge, create a vision for meeting

it, and mobilize stakeholders around that vision. Once that information gets loose within the system, it builds new networks of learning that increase the organization's ability to respond to the next challenge. Therefore, high-performing leaders recognize that one of their most important roles in volatile times is to serve as the "nerve center" and prime mover for information sharing.

A Parting Message: Complexity Plus Complexity Equals Chaos

There's an old joke that goes like this: Three people—a farmer, a surgeon, and a manager—are debating which is the world's oldest profession. (No, it's not what you think.) The farmer says, "The bible says that God gave Adam the animals and plants to tend. Therefore, farming is the world's oldest profession." The surgeon chimes in, "But before that, God took a rib out of Adam to make Eve. Therefore, surgery is the world's oldest profession." Wisely, the manager says, "Yes, but the first thing God did was create order out of chaos. And that means that leadership is the world's oldest profession."

Oldest profession or not, the ultimate purpose of leadership is to bring order out of chaos—to help organizations select the right opportunities from a bewildering array of possibilities. In volatile and chaotic times, this definition is more pertinent than ever. As the world becomes more complex and turbulent, leaders will face increasingly difficult challenges. However, high-performing leaders know that the best solutions are usually the simplest and most highly focused ones. Throwing complex solutions at complex problems is rarely as effective as concentrating on a few fundamentals. Through a "simple" five-step process, the leaders in our study have derived the formula for success: Focus, or fail.

EPILOGUE

WHEN BAD THINGS HAPPEN TO GOOD CORPORATIONS

"The ultimate aim of the hero's quest is neither release nor ecstasy for oneself, but the wisdom and the power to serve others."

—Joseph Campbell

Heroes are fiduciaries for the welfare of their people, for the corporations that undertake useful service, and for the society that embodies collective hopes and aspirations. When bad things happen to good corporations, we see leaders respond and evolve to higher levels to become heroes. Yet, true heroism does not lie only in responding to crisis, however noble that might be, but also in anticipating and planning for its inevitability.

While we may not know the exact nature or timing of crisis events, we can estimate their probability and prepare to meet them. The ten critical elements we've explored thus far have been crafted by leadership heroes who realize that the best preparation for crisis is a day-to-day protocol of thinking and behaving that strengthens resolve, clarifies purpose, and aligns people with each other through a covenant of commitment. Taken together, the ten elements provide a process of stabilization that helps to both reduce the risks of volatility and establish a stable platform from which a response to crisis can be launched effectively. The resiliency of such companies as Southwest, Cisco, Wal-Mart, and the others we've profiled is testimony to the value of such preparation.

Current and past leaders show us how such a response can be developed and implemented. The following are four key rules that all leaders should put into practice in developing an effective plan of response when bad things happen:

1. Understand the threat.
2. Plan for crisis.
3. Adapt on the run.
4. Live the experience of your people.

Rule 1: Understand the Threat

"Trauma is an affliction of the powerless. At the moment of trauma, the victim is rendered helpless by overwhelming force. When the force is that of nature, we speak of disasters. When the force is that of other human beings, we speak of terror and atrocities. Traumatic events overwhelm the ordinary systems of care that give people a sense of control, connection, and meaning."

This passage from Harvard psychiatrist Judith Herman highlights the reality that traumatic events are extraordinary, not because they occur rarely, but rather because they overwhelm the ordinary patterns of adaptation to life. Unlike commonplace misfortunes, traumatic events generally involve threats to life or bodily integrity, or a close personal encounter with violence and death. They confront human beings with the extremes of helplessness and terror. They can shatter the attachments of family, friendship, work, and community. Most profoundly, they undermine the belief systems that give meaning and value to human experience, calling into question all we hope to be as individuals, organizations, and societies.

Traditionally, it was rare to speak of business leadership in terms of trauma, but that is precisely the threat that leaders face in these volatile times. We have often labored under the illusion that bad things—traumatic things—are solely the purview of other sectors of the economy, such as healthcare and the military, or of other, less-developed societies. But, recent events highlight the new realities of an intensely networked and vulnerable global economy. The first step in addressing crisis in these times is recognizing and accepting the new traumatic possibilities. Such recognition, in turn, requires updating and revising standard crisis action plans.

Rule 2: Plan for Crisis

Planning for crisis has been a subject of concern for sometime in business literature, especially preparation for Y2K. Such planning and preparation helped stave off even more tragedy on Wall Street when the events of September 11 occurred. However, more than IT management is required in the event of severe crisis. A process of comprehensive, mission-driven planning is required that grows from and reinforces the core competitive position of the corporation.

Because of its long experience with the threat of terrorism, severe economic shifts, and environmental disasters—both artificial and natural—the oil industry is a benchmark for how to manage volatility and plan for crisis. Shell, in particular, stands out in an industry that is often reviled, but nevertheless essential. Given the continuing political, economic, and environmental concerns over energy—especially oil—there is a special relevance and, perhaps, irony in learning from their experience.

For Shell, long-term thinking provides the key to success in a turbulent world, where crisis management comes into play every day of the week. Routine scenario-based planning helped Shell's special "Group Planning" staff to forecast huge changes in the worldwide oil economy over the past 30 years.

Europe, Japan, and the United States, they concluded, were becoming increasingly dependent on oil imports, while oil-exporting nations such as Iran, Iraq, Libya, and Venezuela were becoming increasingly concerned with falling reserves. Others, such as Saudi Arabia, were reaching the limits of their ability to invest oil revenues productively. These trends meant that the historically smooth growth in oil demand and supply would give way to supply shortages, excess demand, and a "seller's market" controlled by oil-exporting nations.

Though this analysis did not enable Shell to predict the exact timing of political events and the full impact of societal shifts, such as terrorism and Iraq's aggression, it did prepare the company for their effects. Through strategic scenario development, Shell was able to develop likely operational scenarios and translate them into practical action plans and training programs. These programs were also tied into management reviews on everything from navigation training to drug and alcohol policies to crisis management at sea. They even led to a comprehensive plan of surprise drills on its worldwide fleet of tankers.

All this preparation paid off. One tragic accident in 1995 occurred on the 227,411-ton *Rapana* when a fire in the pump room set off an explosion that killed three people. Instantly, Shell opened a direct communication line to the ship in order to manage the crisis from shore by computer. This strategy had been carefully developed and tested in order to free the captain to focus on the safety of the people on board. Throughout the ordeal, Shell kept communications open through its 24-hour manned crisis center in London. The center is supported by a worldwide GPS and computer-controlled piloting system that enables continuous monitoring and, as in this case, actual ship-piloting intervention. Quick, decisive action, built on a plan that had been tested months in advance, resulted in the smooth evacuation of the ship and the prevention of a disastrous oil spill.

Rule 3: Adapt on the Run

Shell provides a vivid example of how preparation for crisis can stave off or minimize the impact of traumatic events. Joe Liana and his team at UPS provide a vivid example of how to leverage operational strengths to adapt to crisis situations even when you're forced to do so on the run. When events of September 11 thrust Joe into an unanticipated situation, he adapted quickly by leveraging his existing capabilities rather than turning elsewhere.

At first, Joe Liana thought it was just his cell phone acting up. But United Parcel Services Inc.'s district manager for Manhattan grew suspicious as calls to his wife and his office were greeted with busy signals on the morning of September 11. He had taken a rare day off to play golf in Queens, and as he dialed for the umpteenth time, he saw a boy running up to him on the third hole. The World Trade Center had been attacked, the boy cried. Liana had 27 people working there. He threw down his clubs and raced off the course, calling out to his stunned golf partners: "I'm going to Manhattan if I have to swim."

Liana caught one of the last trains to Manhattan that day, then flagged down the first UPS truck he saw to take him to UPS's vast complex on 43rd Street near the Hudson River. Once there, the burly 30-year UPS veteran had wireless messages sent to every driver's computerized clipboard, telling them to call in. Within three hours, he learned that his only casualties were four trucks, crushed in the buildings' collapse. Then he summoned all 4,000 of his employees to 43rd Street. With air traffic halted and many streets closed or impassable, they sorted through tens of thousands of packages, looking for medical supplies, then made 200 deliveries to hospitals, doctors, and pharmacies.

Every shipper, from FedEx Corp. to Emery Worldwide, bounced back relatively quickly from the crisis. Within days, packages were arriving at homes and offices across the U.S., thanks to smart crisis management and Herculean efforts to solve logistical nightmares. However, UPS was more fortunate than rival FedEx because it was less reliant on airplanes for deliveries. A series of key decisions at UPS, the world's largest private shipper, helped to keep its trucks running on time.

What saved UPS was its ability to leverage its powerful operational structure to adapt on the run. Its decentralized systems empower district managers like Liana to make key decisions. This empowerment is part of a comprehensive process of cultural and operational alignment supported by a worldwide computer network that enables managers to pinpoint the location of any package. Strong belief in this system and day-to-day practice in translating it into action gave Joe the confidence to respond as he did and adapt on the run to a dramatically different and, for the first few days, constantly changing set of challenges.

A key to the effective management of crisis is realizing the importance of leveraging what you have in place, not in creating totally new solutions that might drain resources, create confusion, and undermine focus when crisis occurs. As Joe Liana demonstrated, the most important points of leverage in crisis are leaders themselves. This is especially the case when it comes to the most personal and intense consequences of crisis.

Rule 4: Live the Experience of Your People

From Christ to Muhammad and Lincoln to Churchill, great leaders have lived the experience of their people. They do not share the burdens of trauma in the abstract. They move immediately and assertively to the front lines of events to provide direction and resolve. They recognize that the jarring impact of a traumatic event affects both those who are immediate targets as well as those who may initially only be observers.

Experts on trauma and crisis note that such events impact people in three fundamental and powerful ways. First, it threatens both physical safety and the psychological sense of it. Not only do traumatic events typically threaten physical harm, they also can undermine the sense of safety and security for a long time afterwards. In the case of profound posttraumatic stress, such as that exhibited by victims of war, terror, or sustained abuse, the sense of threat can be lifelong. Thus, at the first level, issues of survival and safety must be addressed. Until victims of traumatic events feel a sense of stability and control over the physical realities of their existence, it is virtually impossible to address other needs.

Second, trauma undermines one's sense of reality, creating a sense of disbelief that the event could have occurred, often leading to feelings of culpability and guilt, and to a generalized disbelief in what happened. At this level, a leader's responsibility is one of remembrance and affirmation. "Yes, the event did happen. Yes, it produced suffering. No, you are not responsible. You are valued and will be able to return to a productive and gratifying life." This is the message a leader delivers at stage two and which outlines the process of healing he or she must lead.

The third stage involves reconnection with ordinary life and a reintegration with a community of shared purpose. Here, the leader completes a therapeutic process of rebuilding the corporate community by reaffirming the role and importance of those who were disconnected from it by events outside their control.

This is a complex and involved process that can take time. However, two examples from recent times and September 11 show how leaders can achieve remarkable results. One involves Aaron Feuerstein, a business hero who never considered walking away from crisis , and the other is the indefatigable former Mayor of New York, Rudy Giuliani.

Aaron Feuerstein and Malden Mills

The Malden Mills textile factory in Methuen, Massachusetts, was established by Feuerstein's grandfather in 1907. Aaron Feuerstein has lived in New England all of his life and, when he inherited the business, he maintained his loyalty to his community, keeping it in Massachusetts while many other textile companies abandoned the United States. He knew that the small town of Methuen would turn into a ghost town if he pulled out, taking with him the 2,400 jobs supplied by the Mills.

This loyalty did not come cheap, however, and Malden Mills suffered serious financial troubles during the early 1980s. Even when the company declared bankruptcy, however, Feuerstein did not give up. Rather, he continued investing in his R&D team in order to find a big idea, a product that would revive Malden

Mills's flagging fortunes. The result? A lightweight, new fabric, "Polartec," that appealed to both consumers and clothing manufacturers. Almost overnight such companies as L. L. Bean, Eastern Mountain Sports, Lands' End, Patagonia, and Eddie Bauer were featuring the fabric in their outerwear products and, by 1995, Polartec sales had doubled the revenue for Malden Mills, accounting for half of its $400-million-plus income that year.

It looked like smooth sailing for the company at that point. The townspeople of Methuen felt more secure than ever before, as did Aaron Feuerstein himself. Then everything went terribly wrong. One night during the winter of 1995, a boiler at the factory exploded, causing a raging fire that injured 27 employees and leveled three of the factory's buildings. The local president of the Union of Needletrades, Industrial and Textile Employees, and also an employee at the Mills, described the catastrophe: "I was standing there seeing the mill burn with my son, who also works there, and he looked at me and said, 'Dad, we just lost our jobs.' Years of our lives seemed gone."

In fact, the livelihood of the entire city seemed doomed. The 70-year-old Feuerstein would, many assumed, just collect his insurance money and retire. Or, perhaps he would use this turn of events as an excuse to relocate the business overseas. Anyone who thought this, however, didn't really know the man.

Three days after the fire, Feuerstein gathered more than 1,000 people at a local high school gym and announced, "For the next thirty days—and it might be more—all our employees will be paid their full salaries. By January second, we will restart operations, and within ninety days we will be fully operational." No one could believe it—Feuerstein and the Mills were staying! The gym erupted in cheers and hugs.

The company's customers, including L. L. Bean and others, pledged their support. Within days, $330,000 arrived from various companies, the Bank of Boston, the union, and a local Chamber of Commerce. Letters of support, some with modest donations, came from all over the country.

Feuerstein's initial timeframe estimates proved overly optimistic, however. Ninety days came and went, then another ninety, and another. Rebuilding would take much more time and money than he had anticipated. This did not, however, weaken Aaron Feuerstein's resolve. True to his word, he kept rebuilding until, in September 1997, the company held its grand reopening, almost two years after the explosion. Incredibly, the Mills rehired 97.4 percent of the workers who had lost their jobs due to the fire. At the opening, Feuerstein expressed his aim of calling the last seventy employees back to work soon. He would not rest easy until he had reunited the entire Malden Mills community.

Not every leader shares the history and depth of community connection that set the context for this example of crisis leadership. However, every leader should attempt to develop the same type, if not intensity, of connection. Great leaders know their people; and, therefore, when crisis hits, they know how to address all three levels of need. Feuerstein's initial response in guaranteeing wages met safety and security issues. His direct, hands-on involvement with his employees in restarting operations provided both a vehicle for remembrance and mourning as well as reconnection to and preparation for the reintegration as a community of shared purpose that followed.

Aaron Feuerstein's leadership remains a hallmark of how to live the experience of your people because of the complete cycle of involvement and the personal dedication of will and resources. Rudy Giuliani demonstrated similar characteristics in helping New Yorkers—and Americans in general—cope with the trauma of September 11.

Rudy Giuliani and September 11

Shortly before nine o'clock on Tuesday morning, September 11, 2001, Mayor Rudolph Giuliani was on Fifth Avenue, at Fiftieth Street, on his way to City Hall, when he got word that a plane had crashed into the north tower of the World Trade Center. He sped downtown and got there in time to witness what he subsequently described as "the most horrific scene I've ever seen in my whole life." The Mayor spoke to some of the fire commanders at the scene, including the chief of the department, Peter Ganci, who was killed moments later. In a gruesome irony, the city's new emergency command center was situated directly inside the World Trade Center—not in one of the two towers that were hit, but in a third building, which also lay in ruins by the end of the day. Since that location was obviously unsafe, Giuliani went to a suite of city offices a block away, at 75 Barclay Street, where he and his aides intended to set up an alternative command post.

When the first World Trade Center tower collapsed, debris started to rain down from the ceiling of 75 Barclay, and Giuliani and his aides had to evacuate that building as well. They had just finished an impromptu news conference at Chambers Street and West Broadway, and had begun walking north, when the second tower collapsed. It was at that point that the Mayor of the city of New York, along with everybody else in lower Manhattan, found himself running for his life.

Mayors always rush to the scene of disasters; this is as much a part of the job as submitting budgets and making sure the garbage gets picked up on time. No mayor, however, has ever had to react to a disaster of the magnitude of September 11's, and few could have done so with more forcefulness, or steadiness of purpose, than Giuliani. On the day of the attack, the Mayor spoke publicly at least half a dozen times, the last around midnight, and then he went back to the scene to speak to the rescue teams working through the night. Each time he spoke, he managed to convey at once grief and resolve.

"New York is still here," the Mayor said at one point. "We've undergone tremendous losses, and we're going to grieve for them horribly, but New York is going to be here tomorrow morning, and it's going to be here forever." He described speaking to Ganci, who had been a member of the Fire Department for 33 years, just before he died, and telling him, "God bless you." And he urged the people of the city to try to resume their normal lives without bitterness.

"Hatred, prejudice, and anger are what caused this terrible tragedy, and the people of the city of New York should act differently," he said. "We should act bravely. We should act in a tolerant way. We should go about our business, and we should show these people that they can't stop us." By all accounts, the command center the Mayor eventually did establish, at a location that reporters were asked not to divulge, functioned effectively. "It was magnificent, really," Congressional Representative Jerrold Nadler, a frequent critic of the Mayor, said after attending a meeting there.

Andrew Kirtzman, a political reporter for NYl, the city's cable news channel, was running alongside Giuliani on the morning of the tragedy. Kirtzman described the Mayor as entirely composed, even though, for nearly an hour no one seemed to know where he should go. At one point, Kirtzman recalled, the Mayor bumped into a young police officer. She said something to him, and, like a father, he touched her on the cheek. Eventually, he found a temporary office in a fire station, but since all the crews at the station had already left for the World Trade Center, someone had to jimmy the lock in order to let him in.

"On September 11, when New York staggered and seemed about to fall, its Mayor rose from the ashes to catch and steady it. On that day, and the next, and the next, Rudolph Giuliani was exactly the leader the city needed. He was unstintingly there—at the scene, so close that he was nearly killed when the first tower collapsed. His demeanor—calm, frank, patient, tender, egoless, competent—was profoundly reassuring. He displayed all the right emotions, and he displayed them in just the right way, often by keeping them in check. "City fathers" is an old-fashioned term, seldom used anymore except with a hint of derision. But Giuliani, during this terrible time (was) truly the city's father—strong and kind, firm and comforting."

Rudy Giuliani demonstrated a remarkable understanding of leadership in crisis, particularly the power of remembrance, mourning, and reconnection. The September 11 tragedy is particularly instructive in terms of the "collateral" damage of crisis for those who may not have been directly harmed, but were victimized as family members and friends of those who were lost and as members of the larger community who became aware of their own vulnerability. While portions of the world have lived continuously under the threat of trauma from terror and other sources, the industrialized democracies have been relatively secure, particularly the U.S. September 11 changed that.

Leaders have become more aware than ever before of how interconnected they and their organizations are with their people and the larger society of which they are a part. One of the ironic benefits of traumatic events is the reawakening of the need to maintain and strengthen connections—as both individuals and as organizations—to our immediate personal networks and to the society of which we are a part.

One of the central benefits of preparing for the challenge of "bad things happening to good corporations" is the mindset and strategic position of connectedness it puts us in. It reinforces the need and benefit of following a protocol for leadership action that strengthens resolve and the human connections essential for translating it into action. The ten critical elements we've discussed in this book are used by some of our most outstanding corporate and public leaders to manage the volatility and danger inherent in these often chaotic times. They use these elements in a leadership process to create a platform from which they can both launch effective responses to crisis and transform the threat they represent into an opportunity for growth and progress.

APPENDIX

VOLATILITY LEADERSHIP ASSESSMENT

The mini Volatility Leadership Assessment (VLA) is a first step in helping you assess your organizational and personal readiness to manage the effects of economic volatility. This is a significantly abbreviated version of the full VLA that we use in our leadership seminars and advisory services offered through the Murphy Leadership Institute.

In addition to focusing on specific areas targeted by this mini VLA, we recommend that you read the whole book in sequence to reinforce the continuity of the lessons and to achieve the "synergistic kick" that comes from mastering all ten strategies for leading in volatile and chaotic times.

There are 20 questions, each of which relates to a specific topic and chapter in the book. Each question consists of a statement describing you or your organization, followed by four choices about how well that statement applies to you or your organization. There are no trick questions, and remember that only you will see your score.

When you've completed the assessment, use the scoring section and plot your score on the VLA Scoring Grid. Then consult the Volatility Readiness Guide for interpretations and directions on how to proceed.

1. Processes and projects move efficiently in your organization. Speedbumps (such as inefficient procedures, excessive documentation, duplicated effort) are removed. [*Chapter 1*]

   A. Always C. Occasionally
   B. Frequently D. Rarely

2. When you personally face a business situation with an uncertain outcome, you imagine, anticipate, and prepare for at least three possible outcomes so that you are not surprised by what actually happens. [*Chapter 1*]

   A. Always C. Occasionally
   B. Frequently D. Rarely

3. When a customer terminates the relationship with your organization or chooses one of your competitors over you, someone conducts a thorough analysis, trying to work with the lost customer to figure out why. [*Chapter 2*]

   A. Always C. Occasionally
   B. Frequently D. Rarely

4. Regardless of the department in which you work (e.g., accounting, production, sales, R&D, administration, etc.), you work to understand the needs of, and build partnerships with, customers. [*Chapter 2*]

   A. Always C. Occasionally
   B. Frequently D. Rarely

5. The employees at your organization are loyal, fulfilled, hard-working, passionate, and do not experience conflicts between their own personal self-interest and the interests of the company. [*Chapter 3*]

   A. Always C. Occasionally
   B. Frequently D. Rarely

6. You personally ensure that while your employees may have different skills and perspectives, they understand, agree with, and have passion for the organization's core values. [*Chapter 3*]

   A. Always C. Occasionally
   B. Frequently D. Rarely

7. Your oranization consistently fills key positions with the right people for the job, based on talent, previous success, ability to innovate, and commitment to the organization's values, rather than on political pressures or outdated hiring practices. [*Chapter 4*]

   A. Always C. Occasionally
   B. Frequently D. Rarely

8. When you hire employees for your team or department (even if they're an internal hire), you personally perform a thorough reference check to carefully evaluate whether the candidate has the necessary skills and abilities to accomplish what you need. [*Chapter 4*]

   A. Always C. Occasionally
   B. Frequently D. Rarely

9. Your organization effectively manages its knowledge assets and ensures that people in the organization have the appropriate information they need to excel at their jobs. [*Chapter 5*]

   A. Always C. Occasionally
   B. Frequently D. Rarely

10. You personally ensure that people under your sphere of control actively share their knowledge with appropriate interested parties, and you formally/informally reward such behavior. [*Chapter 5*]

    A. Always C. Occasionally
    B. Frequently D. Rarely

11. Your organization anticipates potential economic downturns and ensures that it has sufficient financial resources to remain competitive. [*Chapter 6*]

    A. Always C. Occasionally
    B. Frequently D. Rarely

12. When faced with cost-reduction challenges, you personally perform a careful examination to ensure that costs you cut do not undermine the value that is delivered to your customers (whether internal or external). [*Chapter 6*]

    A. Always C. Occasionally
    B. Frequently D. Rarely

13. Your organization exhibits a healthy paranoia about the threats presented by current and future competitors, and thus looks to build competitive advantages that cannot be easily imitated, substituted, or acquired. [*Chapter 7*]

    A. Always C. Occasionally
    B. Frequently D. Rarely

14. You are personally aware of how your counterparts at your competitors operate, and you strive to make your work competitively superior in order to generate advantages for your organization. [*Chapter 7*]

    A. Always C. Occasionally
    B. Frequently D. Rarely

15. Your organization's, employees do not feel excessively stressed or anxious, and are able to achieve peak levels of performance. [*Chapter 8*]

    A. Always C. Occasionally
    B. Frequently D. Rarely

16. You are personally vigilant for signs of anxiety and stress among your employees and you take steps to deescalate anxiety and stress as soon as it becomes apparent. [*Chapter 8*]

    A. Always C. Occasionally
    B. Frequently D. Rarely

17. Your organization communicates effectively with employees so the appropriate messages are received as they were intended, and not distorted by gossip, communication breakdowns, or message "fade out." [*Chapter 9*]

    A. Always C. Occasionally
    B. Frequently D. Rarely

18. You personally adapt your communication style and methods (including language, media, setting, etc.) to meet the particular needs of individuals and groups with whom you communicate. [*Chapter 9*]

    A. Always C. Occasionally
    B. Frequently D. Rarely

19. When faced with complex and seemingly overwhelming problems, your organization is able to quickly and smoothly get things under control by focusing on key areas of importance and following a disciplined and orderly plan of action. [*Chapter 10*]

    A. Always C. Occasionally
    B. Frequently D. Rarely

20. When faced with complex and seemingly overwhelming problems, you are personally able to quickly and smoothly get things under control by focusing on key areas of importance and by following a disciplined and ordered plan of action. [*Chapter 10*]

    A. Always C. Occasionally
    B. Frequently D. Rarely

Scoring

1. For all of the odd-numbered questions, count the number of responses for each letter. Count the number of A's you marked, then B's, then C's, then D's.

   Odd-Numbered Questions:
   A_____ B_____ C_____ D_____

2. For all of the even-numbered questions, count the number of responses for each letter. Count the number of A's you marked, then B's, then C's, then D's.

   Even-Numbered Questions:
   A_____ B_____ C_____ D_____

3. For each A, give yourself 5 points. For each B, give yourself 3 points. For each C, give yourself 1 point. For each D, give yourself 0 points.

4. The odd-numbered score represents your Organizational Volatility Readiness. This is a measure of how ready your organization is to survive and thrive in times of volatility.

   Organizational Volatility Readiness Score (total score for odd-numbered numbered questions—maximum score is 50)

   ____

   The even-numbered score represents your Personal Volatility Readiness. This is a measure of your personal readiness to survive and thrive in times of volatility.

Personal Volatility Readiness Score (total score for even-numbered questions—maximum score is 50) ________

5. Plot your Personal and Organizational Volatility Readiness Scores on the VLA Scoring Grid to find your assessment results.

VLA Scoring Grid

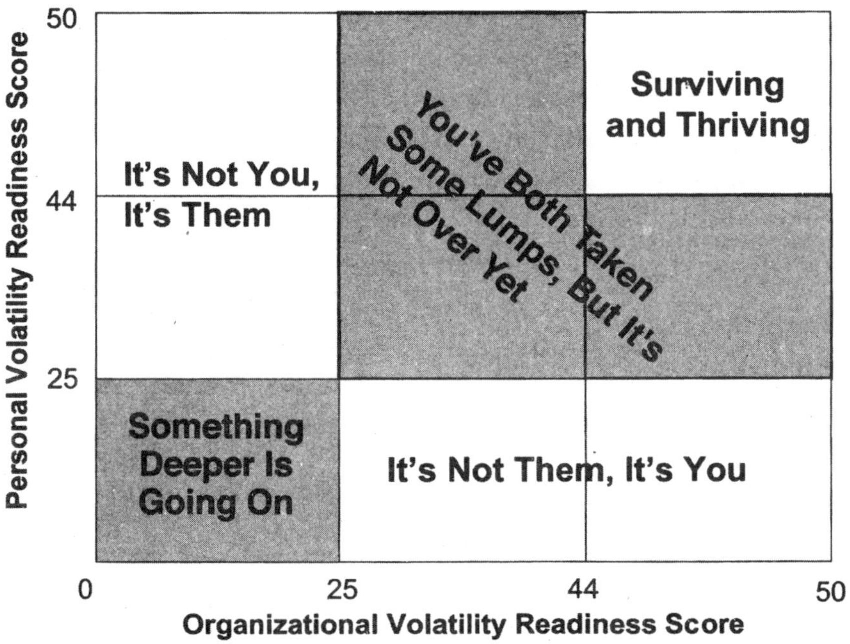

Volatility Readiness Guide

- **Surviving and thriving:** You and your organization are well positioned to emerge from the volatility in much better shape than your competitors. This book will help you fine-tune what you're already doing, and advance even further. Your great risk is "taking your foot off the gas" and allowing your competitors back in the game.

- **You've both taken some lumps, but it's not over yet:** While you and your organization are not "volatility proof," you're within striking distance of making some changes to better position yourselves. This book will help you strengthen the key areas in need of improvement, and help you and your organization achieve new levels of success. Your great risk is sitting idle and not working to strengthen your position while your competitors forge ahead.
- **It's not you, it's them:** You are much better positioned for this current environment than your firm. This may present you with opportunities to really shine, particularly as you are likely to be more advanced than your colleagues. This book will help you take your leadership career to the next level, as well as make some significant improvements in your firm's readiness. Your great risk is not moving to the next level.
- **It's not them, it's you:** Your organization is exhibiting behaviors that are more advanced than your personal behaviors. This book will help you catch up to, and even surpass, your peers to become a truly valued leader. Your great risk is retreating from this personal development challenge and underperforming your potential.
- **Something deeper is going on:** Economic volatility can't explain all of this score. It's likely that you and your organization would be facing some serious challenges regardless of the current economic turbulence. This book will help you turn that situation around and give you the specific steps you need to take to achieve success. Your great risk is becoming overwhelmed by your challenges and not exerting the effort necessary sto develop your leadership skills.

SELECTED REFERENCES

The following provides additional information on some of the issues and leaders referenced in the text.

Chapter 1: Make Haste Slowly

Booker, Katrina. The Chairman of the Board looks back. *Fortune*, May 28, 2001, 62.

Brickley, James A., Clifford Smith, Jr., and Jerold Zimmerman. *Managerial Economics and Organizational Structure*. Boston: Irwin McGraw-Hill, 1997.

Mieszkowski, Katharine. How to speed up your startup. *Fast Company*, 2000, *34*:138.

Murphy, Mark and Emmett C. Murphy. *Leadership Practices and the Management of Disequilibrium Phenomena* (White Paper). Washington, D.C.: The Murphy Leadership Institute, 2001.

Chapter 2: Partner with Customers

Murphy, Emmett C. *Leadership IQ*. New York: John Wiley and Sons, 1996.

Murphy, Mark and Emmett C. Murphy. *The CAP Model as a Mitigator of Organizational Disequilibrium* (White Paper). Washington D.C.: The Murphy Leadership Institute, 2001.

Neff, Thomas J. and James Citrin. Walter Shipley in *Lessons from the Top: The 50 Most Successful Business Leaders in America—and What You Can Learn from Them*. New York: Currency Doubleday, 2001.

Chapter 3: Build a Culture of Commitment

Armstrong, Larry. At SAIC, owners and workers see eye to eye. *Businessweek Online*, June 21, 1999.

Caudron, Shari. Gold-medal HR. *Workforce*, 2000, *79*, no. 9:62,

Coillins and Porras. Built to Last. New York: Harper Business, 1997.

Foundation for Enterprise Development. *Case Study: Science Applications International Corporation*. Fed. Org.

Lewin, Roger and Birute Regine. *The Soul at Work: Listen, Respond, Let Go*. New York: Simon and Schuster, 2000.

Markels, Alex. The wisdom of Chairman Ko. *Fast Company* 29:258.

Chapter 4: Put the Right Person in the Right Place, Right Now

Bennis, Warren and James O'Toole. Don't hire the wrong CEO. *Harvard Business Review*, May-June, 2000.

Bossidy, Larry. 2001. The job no CEO should delegate. *Harvard Business Review*, March, 2001.

Daniels, Cora. To hire a lumber expert, click here. *Fortune*, April 3, 2000.

Murphy, Emmett C. *Leadership IQ*. New York: John Wiley and Sons, 1996.

Row, Heath. Is management for me? That is the question. *Fast Company*, 1998, *13*:50.

Harrington, Ann. How welfare worked for T. J. Maxx. Fortune, November 13, 2000.

Chapter 5: Maximize Knowledge Assets

Glasser, Perry. Armed with intelligence. CIO *Magazine*, 1 August, 1, 1997.

Mendelson, Haim and Johannes Ziegler. *Survival of the Smartest: Managing Information for Rapid Action and World Class Performance*. New York: John Wiley and Sons, 1999.

Stewart, Thomas A. Accounting gets radical. Fortune, April 16, 2001.

Sveiby, Karl-Erik. *What Is Knowledge Management?* Sveiby.com, April, 2001.

Chapter 6: Cut Costs, Not Value

Anders, George. Less burn, more lift. *Fast Company*, 2001, *45*:190

Brealey, Richard A. and Stewart Meyers. *Principles of Corporate Finance*. New York: McGraw-Hill, 2000.

E.C. Murphy, Ltd. Cost-driven downsizing: Implications for mortality and morbidity. *Congressional Record*, 1996.

Gogoi, Pallavi. Cash-rich? So? *Businessweek E-Biz*, March 19, 2001.

Munroe, Ann. Basil Anderson—Campbell Soup. CFO Magazine Online, September 1, 1998

Reason, Tim. 2000 Excellence awards: Larry Carter—Faster than the rest. *CFO Magazine Online*, October, 1, 2000.

Chapter 7: Outposition Your Competitors

Deans of Harvard College. *Wal-Mart Stores, Inc.* Harvard Business School Case Study, 1994.

Kotler, Philip. *Kotler on Marketing: How to Create, Win and Dominate Markets*. New York: The Free Press, 1999.

Kreuger, Pamela. The best way to keep the devil at the door is to be rich. *Fast Company Special Issue: Who's Fast 2000*, November.

Murphy, Mark and Emmett C. Murphy. *Executive Trait Analysis and Research Modeling* (White Paper). Washington, D.C.: The Murphy Leadership Institute, 2001.

Chapter 8: Stir, Don't Shake

Hammonds, Keith. How do we break out of the box we're stuck in. *Fast Company Special Issue: Who's Fast 2000*, November.

Murphy, Emmett C. *The New Murphy's Law*. Worcester, MA: Chandler House Press, 1998.

Murphy, Emmett C. et al. Managing an increasingly complex system. *Nursing Management*, 1997. *28*, no. *10*:33.

Murphy, Mark and Emmett C. Murphy. Cutting healthcare costs through work force reductions. *Healthcare Financial Management*, July 1996, :64.

National Institute for Occupational Safety and Health. *Stress at Work*. Publication No. 99-101. Cincinnati, OH: NIOSH.

Useem, Jerry. A manager for all seasons. *Fortune*, April 30, 2001, :66.

Chapter 9: Cut Through the Noise

Costello, Mary Ann. Stakeholders key to Texas hospital turnaround. *AHA News*, December 11, 2000.

Layne, Anni. How to make your company more resilient. *Fast Company.com*, March 2001.

Pascale, Richard T., Mark Milleman, and Linda Gioja. *Surfing the Edge of Chaos: The Laws of Nature and the New Laws of Business*. New York: Crown Business, 2000.

Chapter 10: Focus or Fail

Murphy, Emmett C. *Forging the Heroic Organization*. Englewood Cliffs, NJ: Prentice Hall, 1994.

Roberts, Paul. Getting it done. *Fast Company*, 2000, *35*:146.

Epilogue: When Bad Things Happen to Good Corporations

Herman, Judith, M.D. *Trauma and Recovery*. New York: Basic Books, 1997, p. 32.

Kolbert, Elizabeth. The best of Rudy Giuliani. *New Yorker*, October 1, 2001.

ABOUT THE AUTHORS

Emmett C. Murphy

Emmett C. Murphy, Ph.D., is a Senior Fellow of the Murphy Leadership Institute. He is the author of the *New York Times* bestsellers *Leadership IQ* and *The Genius of Sitting Bull: Thirteen Heroic Strategies for Today's Business Leaders*. Dr. Murphy was formerly Chairman and CEO of E. C. Murphy, Ltd., the management consulting subsidiary of VHA, Inc., the world's largest business services and healthcare alliance. Dr. Murphy's clients have included IBM, Chase Manhattan, Hewlett-Packard, the Department of Defense, and Johns Hopkins and Stanford University Hospitals. He has held academic and consulting positions with the Harvard Business School, M.I.T.'s Sloan School of Management, the American Management Association, Booz-Allen Hamilton, and the London University, among others. He holds a Ph.D. in Organizational Psychology from the State University of New York, with postdoctoral certificates in Operations Research from the Massachusetts Institute of Technology and in Psychological Counseling from the Upstate Medical Center of S.U.N.Y.

Mark Andrew Murphy

Mark Andrew Murphy, M.B.A., is President and CEO of the Murphy Leadership Institute. He has published extensively on leadership and organizational change, and his work has appeared in *USA Today*, the *Wall Street Journal*, and *the Congressional Record*, among others. He is the winner of the Healthcare Financial Management Association's international Helen Yerger Award for outstanding research contributions to the field of financial management. Mr. Murphy was also a pioneer in researching the effects of corporate downsizing and first discovered the link between reductions-in-force and mortality rates in hospitals. Mr. Murphy's clients have included such organizations as DuPont, Hewlett-Packard, Blue Cross/Blue Shield, William M. Mercer, Kemper Insurance Companies, SmithKline Beecham, Blockbuster Video, Yale Medical Center, and the Surgeon General. He holds an M.B.A. from the University of Rochester and is a member of Beta Gamma Sigma.

The Murphy Leadership Institute

The Murphy Leadership Institute works to increase the leadership intelligence of managers, executives, boards, and organizations through training, assessment, and advisory services. The Murphy Leadership Institute sponsored and directed one of the largest leadership studies in two decades, and continuously translates its research into best-practice leadership solutions. The Murphy Leadership Institute provides state-of-the-art research and experientially-proven strategies in all of its leadership offerings, including training courses, seminars, leadership and organizational assessments, and published materials. Contact us via the following.

Murphy Leadership Institute
1025 Connecticut Avenue, NW, Suite 1012
Washington, D.C. 20036
866-252-LEAD
www.MurphyLeadershipInstitute.com

INDEX

D